SWING TRADING:

© **Copyright 2019 - All rights reserved.**

The content contained within this book may not be reproduced, duplicated or transmitted without direct written permission from the author or the publisher.

Under no circumstances will any blame or legal responsibility be held against the publisher, or author, for any damages, reparation, or monetary loss due to the information contained within this book. Either directly or indirectly.

Legal Notice:

This book is copyright protected. This book is only for personal use. You cannot amend, distribute, sell, use, quote or paraphrase any part, or the content within this book, without the consent of the author or publisher.

Disclaimer Notice:

Please note the information contained within this document is for educational and entertainment purposes only. All effort has been executed to present accurate, up to date, and reliable, complete information. No warranties of any kind are declared or implied. Readers acknowledge that the author is not engaging in the rendering of legal, financial, medical or professional advice. The content within this book has been derived from various sources. Please consult a licensed professional before attempting any techniques outlined in this book.

By reading this document, the reader agrees that under no circumstances is the author responsible for any losses, direct or indirect, which are incurred as a result of the use of information contained within this document, including, but not limited to, — errors, omissions, or inaccuracies.

Description

Introducing

Why is Swing Trading Better Than Day Trading?

The Daily Routine of a Swing Trader

How Greeks Predict Option Pricing

Swing Trading with Call Options

Candlestick Chart Patterns and Technical Indicators

Fundamental Analysis

Technical Analysis

Watch for Counter Trends

Breakout & Breakdown trading

Predicting the Market

Having the Right Mindset for Trading

The Secret of Profitable Trading

Commandments of Swing Trading

The Top Mistakes That Beginners Make

Conclusion

Description

The amazing thing about trading and competing in the stock market is the sheer number of opportunities available. At any given time, there are new profitable positions that are waiting to be discovered. If you genuinely enjoy reading about new companies and current events, then it will be easier to identify opportunities as they appear.

Remember that the best way to find opportunities is to research stocks and sectors that you already have a personal interest in. The knowledge you have already is a useful tool for staying ahead of the market. If you have an interest in cars, then you'll probably enjoy reading about automotive companies; what new car models are being introduced and how do you think they will perform? If you have an interest in computers and tech; what types of technology have you read about that you think could be groundbreaking? Out of all the new companies producing these technologies, which ones have the most promising fundamentals, and are more likely to succeed? If you approach to research this way, then you'll no doubt find opportunities for stocks to trade and invest with.

This book gives a comprehensive guide on the following:

- Why is Swing Trading Better Than Day Trading?
- The Daily Routine of a Swing Trader
- How Greeks Predict Option Pricing
- Swing Trading with Call Options
- Candlestick Chart Patterns and Technical Indicators
- Fundamental Analysis
- Technical Analysis
- Watch for Counter Trends
- Breakout & Breakdown trading
- Predicting the Market
- Having the Right Mindset for Trading
- The Secret of Profitable Trading
- Commandments of Swing Trading
- The Top Mistakes That Beginners Make... AND MORE!!!

Introducing

The Definition of Swing Trading

There is a lot of confusion out there about what swing trading really is. So, let me be very clear on what it is.

Swing trading is a short-term trading style that involves you taking a position in the financial markets and staying with it for a number of days, perhaps weeks. So, you could watch American Express stock today and decide that you are going to buy it, then after you place your trade, you let it stay for a day or two, perhaps even more depending on how fast the market action is and the time frame you are watching.

Swing trading is different from other types of trading such as position trading, day trading, high frequency trading or scalping mainly because of the period of time that a trade is held. On one hand, some trading styles such as position trading allow you to take a position and then hold it for a longer period of time such as a couple of months or even years. On the other hand, a style such as scalping can involve holding a position for a few minutes, perhaps even seconds. Therefore, a good way to think about swing trading is, a style that strikes a balance between both sides, offering more flexibility.

As a swing trader, you are mainly looking to profit from short term price changes or what is known as price swings in the markets. Now that we have fully defined what swing trading is, let us compare it to "Day trading."

Swing trading vs. Day trading

As I said before, many people who are new to trading ask themselves, "What is the difference between Swing trading and Day trading?" So, let's talk about it. Day trading is a completely different trading style. And the difference between the two comes down to the length of time that positions are held. Day trading is a trading style in which you execute a number of positions in a day, but at the end of the day, you close all of them out. So, you may open a number of trades, say 10 of them in a day, but at the end of the day, you are flat.

You will never find a day trader holding a position overnight, the way you may find swing traders or position traders doing. A day trader prefers to take small daily gains from the market consistently but not hold his positions for any longer than a day. Because of this, you will often find day traders seeking opportunities in short time frames such as one minute, five minutes, ten minutes or even 30 minutes.

If you think about it, day trading is more like a day job. As a matter of fact, most hot shot day traders simply regard it as their main source of income.

Swing trading is regarded as more of a part time activity. In swing trading, you will be typically looking at longer time frames such as 3 hours, 4 hours, daily or weekly to spot swing trading opportunities. Therefore, this type of trading can be adopted by people who are or already employed in a different job.

If for instance you are a swing trader who is looking at a 4-hour chart to trade, this means that a single candlestick in a candlestick chart will be formed every four hours. This means that you only need to check up your chart every four hours to see what is going on. So, if you are an employee, even with a busy schedule, my guess is you can still afford to check up a chart every four hours. So, this type of trading style can suit you.

Another thing to keep in mind is that, since day trading involves placing trades every now and then, the natural ups and downs of the markets can end up being very stressful indeed. A small mistake in this type of trading can end up wiping you out on all your profits. So, day trading can only suit you if you are someone who very disciplined and can withstand short term ups and downs in your portfolio.

Swing trading allows you take a more laidback approach. You can place a trade and walk away from your computer and not have to worry about it until may be the next day. So, if your goal is to seek a source of income that is more passive, then swing trading is the way to go. It is also good for you if you are a person of mild temperament who doesn't like lots of action.

Truth be told, none of these trading styles is better than the other. It is just a matter of picking the trading style that fits you as a person and your current situation in life. You may want to consider the following before you make a decision:

- The amount of time that you can set aside for trading: If you are a busy person, you may want to consider swing trading.
- The amount of money that you have: Day trading may require that you start out with a lot of money since you will end up being dependent on it for your means of livelihood.

- Your personality: If you are more of a person who likes to take things nice and slow, you may want to stay away from day trading and opt for swing trading instead.

- Risk tolerance: Day trading is for you if you can withstand watching several trades going against you and still maintain your calmness. Swing trading is better if you are more of the calculating type who can only stand taking a loss once in a while.

- Trading experience: Trading experience matters a lot in trading. If you are new to trading, you may need to start as a swing trader and take your time to learn the ropes. After you start mastering the business, you can then slowly graduate to day trading. Day trading is meant for competent professionals who have a lot of experience in this business and therefore know what they are doing.

Now that you have fully understood what Swing trading is and how different it is from Day trading; it is time that we began looking into a number of Swing trading strategies that you can apply.

Why is Swing Trading Better Than Day Trading?

As you are looking through these two options, you may notice that swing trading seems very similar to working with day trading. While there are some similarities between these two, and there are many times that they will use some of the same strategies in the same way, they are two very different forms of investing. In many cases, investors tend to favor working with swing trading because it gives them more time to make decisions and can help them to earn more profit on each trade. Some of the advantages of working with swing trading compared to day trading include:

- *Temperament:* If you are not a fan of making split-second decisions, then swing trading may be a better option for you.
- *Availability:* If you don't have all day to watch the market and do the research and trading, then swing trading is a better option for you.
- *Lifestyle balance:* Day trading can take up a lot of time and can take away from the balance of your work and your leisure activities. Swing trading doesn't cause quite a much of a hassle.

- *Financial demands:* Swing trading is often less demanding financially when compared to day trading. This is especially true when you are a beginner who doesn't have a lot of money to invest.
- *Less idle time:* You won't need to sit around and wait as long for a trade or an alert before you can set it up.

These are just a few of the benefits that you can get when you decide to get started with swing trading rather than relying on day trading. Let's take a closer look at each of these reasons to get a better understanding of why swing trading may be the strategy that you need.

Temperament

If you are someone who doesn't really like to make snap decisions, then day trading is often not the best idea, and swing trading can work better for you. One advantage of this kind of trading is that you have more time luxury than others. You can take some more time to consider the trades that you want to take before you make a trade. You can use a variety of tools and analyze the trade a bit before using the strategy. You also have more time to determine your rewards and your risks, which can be very important when you want to be a successful trader.

Swing trading is a much better option for those who see themselves as methodical thinkers, the ones who like to plan out a trade in advance, the ones who like to determine the best entry points, analyze the upside and the downside, and the ones who want to settle on an exit strategy. Moreover, they want to have plenty of time to do all of this before they push to either purchase or sell the security they want to trade.

To keep it simple, if you are someone who likes to have some time to figure out if a specific approach is the best for you, then swing trading is the best option. In some cases, you may find that you are well adapted to doing both swing trading and day trading. But, for those who want to have more time to think through their decisions and those who want to be able to enjoy the trading a bit more, then swing trading is the better option.

Availability

The next thing that you need to look at is your availability. All of the exchanges in North America are going to open up at 9:30 am Eastern Time and then will go until 4 pm Eastern Time as well. The chances that you get to trade outside of these hours are known as pre-market and after-market, but trading during these periods is usually not recommended because there is less predictability and higher volatility during these times.

The amount of time that you have to trade the market during certain times of the day can depend on a few factors but mostly on where you live or your specific time zone. If you live on the west coast, for example, you would have to trade between 6:30 and 1:00 each day. This may work a bit for you because you could get a few hours of trading in before heading to work.

But, if you live on the east coast and you have to be at work by 9:00 in the morning, you may find that there aren't many hours for you to trade with. In this case, swing trading may be the best option for you. You will have the luxury of trading in the evening or even during your lunch break. You can use this time to check your stocks, view the market action, and then get back to work.

With day trading, you would have to watch the market all day. But, with swing trading, you could just check in on occasion and see how the market is doing when it works for you. Just make sure that you put in the right entry and exit orders. If you do this, then the price movements of the securities will come to you and fill your orders during the day, even when you are doing other obligations during the day.

Lifestyle Balance

Now, we are going to spend some time looking at how swing trading is better for a lifestyle balance. Everyone is different when it comes down to how much time they want to set aside for work, and how much they want to set aside for play. Some like to work all of the time, but most people like to have at least a little time for fun activities in their days. You also have to figure out how much time you need to devote to your family and other commitments on top of the work that you want to do with trading.

Again, one of the advantages of doing swing trading is that there is a lot of flexibility for the trader to enjoy. You don't have to sit in front of the computer all day, so you get some freedom to come and go. Yes, you do need to sit down each day and review your position, look for some new opportunities to take care of, and pay attention to what the market is doing. But you don't have a requirement for what time to sit and watch the market, and you don't have to stay there all day long.

Financial Demands

With swing trading, you won't need to have as much money ready to get started. Ideally, you will start at about $5000 in your account. If you can, it is better to start with more, but it is possible to start with less depending on the trades that you want to do. Just remember that the less capital you put into your trading account to start, the more limited number of choices you will have when it comes to stocks you can trade with.

If you want to open up a margin account, the amount of capital that you need to start can be a little bit less. Government regulations state that these margin accounts need to have a minimum of $2000 in them. The deposit can be done in cash or in other negotiable securities, like bonds or stocks that you hold onto. You will have to talk with your broker about using those first.

When compared to doing day trading, the US requires that you deposit a minimum of $25,000 in the account before you can even take a look at trading. This amount is pretty high, and it is going to be more than what most people are able to do. This alone can be a big advantage when it comes to trading with swing trading.

Less Idle Time

Most people have better things to do than just sit around and wait to see something happen. You have other obligations, work, chores, family, and more that you want to spend your time on. But, when you are a day trader, you will have to spend a lot of time sitting, watching, and waiting in between all of your tradeable opportunities, and this can be a lot of wasted time, which most people don't want.

When it comes to swing trading, though, you can still monitor your positions while doing some of your other responsibilities and duties for the day. You don't have to keep yourself tied to a computer screen, waiting to see an alert from your scanning program, or waiting for a big market event to take place that will help you see that a security is going to move in one direction or another. This can free up a lot of your time compared to what day traders have to deal with to make any profits.

As you can see, there are a lot of benefits that come with swing trading. It is a short-term strategy, so you don't have to stay in the market for too long, but it still provides you with the benefits that you are looking for when you want to earn a good profit in the process. You still get more time to do the trades, you don't have to stay connected to a computer all day, and swing trading is usually seen as an easier option compared to other trading strategies.

The Daily Routine of a Swing Trader

Swing traders differ from investors in various ways. Investors buy shares and hold on to them for lengthy periods of time. They often hope to generate annual returns, like 10% to 20% per annum on their investments. This is a different approach from traders who enter the markets and exit after a very short while. Traders hope to make small but frequent profits in the course of a few days or weeks. Their aim is to make between 10% - 15% or more each month. This translates into big returns over time.

Swing traders use both fundamental analysis and technical analysis to determine stocks with an upward trend and with momentum. A swing trader's work includes the identification of financial instruments such as stocks that have a well-defined trend.

The aim of a swing trader is to purchase securities when the prices are low, hold the securities for a couple of days, and then exit when the prices are high. This way, they exit trades profitably, and it is the method that they use to earn their profits. It makes sense to enter trades when prices are low and then sell when the prices go up.

As a retail trader, you may be at a disadvantage compared to professional traders. Professional traders are generally more experienced, have a lot of leverage, access to more information, and pay lower commissions. However, you do have some advantages in some instances because you are not limited to the risks that you can take, size of investment, and types of trades. As a retail swing trader, you need to ensure that you have all the knowledge necessary to take full advantage of the markets.

Trading Techniques

Swing trading techniques are easy to learn. They are also straightforward and simple to demonstrate. After learning these techniques, it is advisable to put them to practice for a couple of days until you get confident enough to trade live. If your practice trades were largely successful, then trading the real markets will also likely prove to be successful.

As a swing trader, you do not have to focus your energies using complicated formulas and learning complex techniques. You also do not need to buy and hold stocks or other financial instruments like currencies. Instead, you only need your trading charts.

Beginning of the Trading Day

As a swing trader, you need to be up early before the markets open. Most traders are awake by 6.00 in the morning and start preparing for their trading day. The few moments just before the opening of the markets are crucial as you get the feel of the market.

One of the first things that you need to focus on is finding a potential trade. You should spend your time finding securities that are on a sure trend. Another thing you should focus during these early morning moments is creating a watch list of stocks and securities. Also, check out all your other positions.

Current News and Developments

You should take time in the morning to catch up with the latest developments and news, especially those that directly impact businesses. One of the best sources of financial and business news is CNBC, which is a cable news channel. Another great source of market information is the website www.marketwatch.com. This is an informative website that provides the latest and most reliable market news.

As a swing trader, you need to be on the lookout for three things in the news. These are different sentiments in various market sectors, current news reports such as earnings reports, and the overall market outlook. Are there sectors that are in the news? Is the news considered good or bad? What significant thing is happening in other sectors? If something significant or of concern happens, then you are likely to come across it in the news.

Identifying Potential Trades

So how do you find trades that you'd be interested in? As a swing trader, you may want to find a catalyst. A fundamental catalyst will enable you to enter a trade with sufficient momentum. Then all you will need is technical analysis to confirm your exit and profit points.

1. Special Opportunities

There are different ways of entering the market. One of these is to find a great opportunity with so much potential. Great opportunities can be found through companies planning an IPO, those ready to file for bankruptcy, situations of takeovers, buyouts, insider buying, mergers, acquisitions, and restructuring. These and other similar events provide excellent trading opportunities, especially for swing traders.

To find these opportunities, you need to check out the SEC website or filings from companies. Certain forms such as 13-D and S-4 contain all the relevant information that you need. You can also subscribe to the website www.SECFilings.com so as to receive notifications whenever companies file reports. While these opportunities carry some inherent risks, the possible rewards are too great to ignore.

2. Sector or Industry Opportunities

Apart from the rare opportunities, we also have opportunities that are specific to a given sector. These are opportunities that you will find on certain websites regarding sectors whose performance is well above average. For instance, we can determine that sectors such as energy are doing exceptionally well by observing energy ETFs. There are certain sectors that pose a high risk but have high returns and can be very profitable.

3. Chart Breaks

We can also rely on chart breaks to find opportunity. Chart breaks are especially suitable for swing traders. Chart breaks are really stocks or securities that have been traded so heavily such that they are very close to major resistance or support levels. As a swing trader, you will search for opportunities out there by identifying patterns indicating breakdowns or breakouts.

These identifying patterns can be Gann or Fibonacci levels, Wolfe Waves, channels, and triangles. However, please note that these chart breaks are only useful when there is huge interest in the stock. This way, you can easily enter and exit trades. Therefore, whenever you note this chart breaks, you should also focus on factors such as price and volumes.

Securities Watch List

One of the things that you really should embark on is building a list of stocks or other securities to watch closely. The stocks that should constitute this list include those with a great chance at high volumes and upward price movement. It should also include stocks with a major catalyst.

Checking Your Current Positions

It is important to keep tabs on your current positions. You probably have other trades so take a look at these and see if there is anything needed on your part. This is something that you should focus on early before the trading day begins. You should review these positions with the benefit of foresight based on the information obtained from news sources and online sites. See if any news items will affect your current positions.

Checking this out is pretty easy and straight forward. All that you need to do is to enter the stock symbol into websites such as www.news.google.com. This will reveal plenty of essential information that you need to be successful. Should you come across any material information that can directly affect your trades, then consider what you should do, such as adjusting the different points like take profit and stop loss.

Market Hours

Now that the markets are open, it is time to get busy as a trader. During this time, you will mostly be trading and watching your screen. Check the market makers of the day and also be aware of any fake bids and asks.

Find a viable trade and apply all the skills and knowledge you have acquired to identify entry and exit points. There are plenty of techniques you can apply to arrive at these points. Think about Fibonacci extensions, for example. These can help you identify entry and exit points; you can also use price by volume and resistance levels.

As the trading day proceeds, you may need to make certain adjustments to your positions. These adjustments will depend on a number of factors. However, it is not advisable to adjust positions once you enter a trade, especially if you are planning on taking on additional risks. If you have to make adjustments, then it is better to focus more on adjusting the take profit points and stop loss levels.

After Hours

Most swing traders are largely inactive after the normal trading day is over. At this point in time, the market is not liquid at all and the available spread not suitable to enter any trades. Therefore, take this time to do some evaluation of your earlier trades and your positions. Examine your trades and see where you could do better. Focus on any open positions you may have and consider all material events that could have some effect on your positions.

Summary

To be an efficient trader, you need to have a routine. You should learn to wake up early before the beginning of the trading day and to get prepared. You also need to automate as many processes as possible. The crucial step is learning how to set up your workstation and your trading computer. Doing this ensures that you are totally ready for the trading day.

As a trader, you really need to learn how to separate charting from trading. There needs to be a different platform for charting, and in our case, www.tradingview.com comes highly recommended. It is just when you are ready to begin trading that you will log onto your trading platform.

There is a good reason for this. If you use the same platform for both charting and trading, you may fall into the trap of impulse decision. You will clearly view your orders right in front of your face. This will create a sense of panic and urgency, and you may do things in a hurry. When they are on different platforms, you create a thin layer that prevents impulsive action.

It is advisable to learn how to use templates a lot more effectively. This helps especially with the charting. Charting becomes an extremely effective and efficient process when you come up with different templates with varying colors. For instance, you can come up with a different color for resistance and support levels and other tools. The next time that you trade, it will be easy to track each tool individually based on its color code.

Also, remember to come with relevant alerts. Some traders prefer using multiple screens in order to monitor multiple developments at the same time. Instead of multiple screens, you can choose to create specific alerts so that should something relevant occur somewhere, then you will get to hear about it on time. Alerts are crucial and will ensure that you get to find out when there is a price movement and so on.

You can use the weekends to plan the coming trading week. You can do this without the worry or concern of active markets. You can also take the time to come up with different trading strategies and styles that can help you attain your trading goals.

Think up of different situations that can arise as you trade and then come up with suitable solutions for each. This way, should any situation happen in the course of the trading week then you will be well prepared to handle it. Sometimes, though, you may feel the need to use a trading template already designed. These can be found online and are easy to download. However, you can also come up with your own trading plan and strategy to implement. In brief, you should always enter a trade with a plan in hand. This means that you should plan your trade and then trade your plan.

How Greeks Predict Option Pricing

The Greeks, as they are known as, can be daunting mathematics filled with formulas necessary to measure an options position exposure to risk. Fortunately for you and me, today these are calculated for us on trading platforms used to trade options. I'll define each of the Greeks, but we are going to focus on Delta. Delta is the option Greek you will want to become familiar with because it helps you to understand how an option's premium will rise or fall in comparison to the price of the underlying stock.

Since our main goal in trading options is to make money, the most important thing you need to know ahead of time is how the security we're trading will move at price. When it comes to options, this knowledge is found in "Delta."

Delta is a mathematical formula to measure the magnitude of change of an option's price as the underlying Stock moves in price. Here is what that formula looks like, but don't worry if it makes your eyes cross, your broker will do the calculations and list each options current delta within the trading platform. You will merely need to look it up, know what the number means and how it affects the trade.

- ABC stock trading at $50
- A call option with a Delta reading of .60

☐ A .60 Delta reading for a call option for ABC stock would mean that for every $1 upward move in ABC's stock price, the call option premium would increase by .60 cents or $60 (.60 x 100 = $60).

☐ A -.60 Delta reading on a put option for ABC stock would mean that for every $1 downward move in ABC's stock price, the put option premium would increase by .60 cents or $60 (.60 x 100 = $60).

However, the Delta will also work against you should the stock move in the opposite direction by the same amount. A call with a .60 delta will lose $60 in value for every $1 downward move in the underlying stock and a put option with a -.60 Delta would lose $60 in value for every upward move in the underlying stock.

How to Use Delta to Calculate Potential Gains

Using the Delta alone you will be able to guesstimate (you'll have to use Gamma to be accurate) how many $1 moves a stock must make to double or triple your investment, and when you might want to sell the option for maximum profit if the underlying security is likely to reach the move you are expecting. Here is another example of a practical application:

- ABC stock trading at $50
- Call option Delta reading at .60
- Call option premium at $4.00

How many .60 ($60 increase in option price) moves would it take to double your money? The option increases by $60 for every $1 move up in the underlying stock, so it would roughly take a $6 move upward at ABC's stock price to double your money ($4.00/.60 = 6.666) ($60 x 6.66 = $399.6) our option premium price would need to be at $7.99 before we sold it to double your investment.

You might ask yourself if ABC stock is likely to make a $6 move upwards or lower your sell target. Would this information be helpful in trading options? Absolutely! Knowing where you are going will aid you in knowing when to sell for greater profits on a trade, without this knowledge you would be hoping and praying it doubled when in fact from the beginning it was not likely to double at all.

What happens to traders who don't practice this calculation and apply it to their trades? They hold on to a declining asset, hoping it will return and surpass the previous highs, when in fact it has hit its support and resistance levels and is now headed in the opposite direction. By the time it returns to those levels again, the option is near its expiration and time decay has substantially diminished the option price, or it's almost worthless. Don't let this happen to you; practice the calculation on any options you are considering buying. You might not get it down your first couple of trades, but you will soon see the value, and you will have an edge that the majority of options traders fail to understand.

Now you are ready to learn about Delta's buddy, Gamma. While Delta is usually sufficient, adding Gamma to the calculation will make your Delta more accurate instead of just roughly accurate. Yet, if adding Gamma blows up your brain, you can do good with Delta and add Gamma later if you want a more accurate sell target calculation.

The Only Other Greek You'll Ever Need is Gamma

Gamma measures how much the option's Delta changes in response to the changes in price to the underlying asset. More simply stated, Gamma shows you how much the Delta will change with each $1 move in the underlying stock price. Here is another example so you can fully understand how it makes delta calculations more accurate:

If Gamma is reading 0.05, it means Delta will increase by .05 for every dollar move. In our earlier example, Delta was at .60 and meant the premium would increase by $60 for every $1 move up in the underlying stock price. We calculated that we would need a $6 move in the stock price to double our investment with a current option premium of $4 when we add Gamma to the mix it changes our calculations to the better. Using Gamma, we know that for every $1 move up our delta calculation will increase .05 and our profit on the option if the stock moves up $6 is now $435 vs. 399.60 when we merely use our Delta calculation. It's not necessary to use Gamma if you are fine with Delta calculations only, but you can see that you could adjust your sell target to $425, $430 of $433, etc., earning slightly more from your investment by using Gamma.

Swing Trading with Call Options

Now it's time to go into the "how's" of swing trading. This chapter will discuss how to swing trade stocks and options, as well as how to look at charts to find patterns, and how to make a trading plan. Once you are finished with this chapter, please, don't just leave the book and start trading! Instead, take what you've learned and use some practice simulators to do some practice trades. You should spend time practicing before using your money to swing trade.

How to Swing Trade

Let's review some of the basics of swing trading. Swing trading is buying an asset during a "swing" in the chart. If you're looking at a chart, the swings are those short rises up and the short rises back down. They make the small hills and valleys in the chart. They're pretty small, so you're not looking for a larger trend, you're simply looking for those changes that occur during a week-long period. In swing trading, you need to analyze the chart, find the support and the resistance of the asset, and then determine a good area to enter and exit the trade. Your analysis will also show you where to place your stop-loss. A stop-loss is incredibly important because it can help you prevent you from over-investing in the trade. This sounds really simple, but there's more to it, so this section will cover these topics.

How to find the support and resistance

As a swing trader, you should sell the asset before it reaches the resistance. Resistance is the highest point reached before a reversal or swing low. It is the point at which most people start selling their stock, and thus, it starts a new dip in the trend. Support is the lowest point it reaches before going up. Support is the point at which many people start buying the stock, so the stock prices rise.

Take, for example, a person throwing a ball in the air. The point of your hands holding the ball before the throw is your support point. It is the lowest point that the ball reaches before you throw it. After throwing the ball, the highest point in its arch, before it falls again, is the resistance. When swing trading, you want to sell the asset before it reaches resistance.

The reason why you want to sell your stock before you reach resistance is because resistance is the area where most people start selling. This means that your stock price might dip soon after so it's a good idea to sell before you hit resistance. Resistance can be calculated by analyzing a chart. Look at the chart's history for the last year. What is the highest point the stock is valued at, and how consistent is that? For example, if you're trading stock ABC, and you look back at their last 12 months on the market, you want to find at which points they were selling the highest. Maybe for a couple of months out of the year, the highest value the stocks had was $20. If it's a consistent pattern, then that is your resistance level. It's unlikely that the stock will break out of this pattern. This means that you want to plan your exit before this number is reached.

Resistance can be a useful tool for determining the peak price of a stock, but so can be other tools like moving averages. Whichever tool you choose in order to find the topmost point, make sure you stick with it and don't trade beyond that point. One thing with swing trading is that you won't know if the stock will go beyond the resistance point, but you still need to have your exit plan and follow it.

Support is the point at which you may want to buy the stock. Remember, support is the historically lowest point on the chart where the stock has been placed. Using the same strategy as the resistance one, you want to look at a chart's history for the last twelve months and find the areas where the stock has traded the lowest. For example, if you're trading stock ABC and you see that for the last year, the stock never dipped below $10, then that would be your support line. You don't want to trade below these points. In fact, it would be better to enter the trade somewhere a bit higher and ride the wave of the swing to your exit point. Remember, the goal is to find small profits in a short period of time, so once you've planned your exit within a few days, take it. Even if the market is doing well, it's better to bow out early than mistime it and lose your profits.

Again, just like with resistance, you can combine the support line with the moving averages tool to help you find the points that are best to enter in. Most charts that you'll find online will include the choice to see the moving averages for both the highs and the lows. You can use resistance and support to help you calculate from there.

Now that you understand the basics of resistance and support, it's time to practice. Find a sample stock chart online. You can use stockchart.com or other websites. Stock charts are free, so you don't need to pay to see the data. Using your sample chart, draw your lines for support and resistance during a given point in time. As you draw your lines, keep some things in mind: support and resistance lines are often slanting, going in the direction of the trend. They're not always horizontal, though they can be if the market is neutral and there is no prevailing trend. Find the areas on the chart where there are multiple touches. For example, maybe the lines touch the price point $120 multiple times in the last year. This is a good place to put your resistance or support line (depending on how the rest of the chart looks). Within these two lines is now your zone for purchasing. You can find an area that you would enter the trade and an area that you would exit based on what you're seeing. This is just a practice, furthermore you have the benefit of seeing a past chart.

To apply this to a future trade, try the same thing, but this time analyze the charts of three different securities you're interested in. Map out your support and resistance, and then choose a place that you would enter into the trade and where you would like to exit the trade. Remember to exit before resistance, and enter after support. Using a simulator (remember, practice first), or just by following the chart for a couple of days, you can see how your trade would have panned out if you had put money on the trade. Keep practicing this way, and you'll be able to find patterns in the markets. Since, as mentioned before, history repeats itself when it comes to trades. You can also adjust your strategies regarding resistance and support after some trial and error.

Remember to take lots of time to practice trades with a simulator, or just by following your own charts for a while before using your capital. Once you're ready to actually start trading, you want to follow the strategy that you developed, and map out your resistance and support. In the next section, we're going to talk about pinpointing the best areas to enter and exit a trade.

Candlestick Chart Patterns and Technical Indicators

These patterns are really easy to detect when you're looking at candlestick charts while utilizing the correct technical indicator. Now, using technical indicators isn't always easy, but it's pretty much a 2-step process:

1. Apply Technical Indicators To The Price Of Your Stock- Here, you'll be applying technical indicators (which are simply math formulae) which will show you whether or not the stock is displaying buy or sell signals.

Technical indicators generally remove all subjectivity from analyzing a chart pattern. Technical indicators are one of two kinds- trending and non-trending.

- Trending technical indicators will show you the most significant changes in a given direction and mostly filter out the chart noise (irrelevant changes which don't contribute to the overall trend.) Now, this can easily happen over a few days, and the indicators will help measure the trends as well as signal when the trend is about to reverse, which will let you sell out at an ample time.

- Non-trending technical indicators tend to work with the buyers and sellers of a security. It determines how much the strength of the other investors in the market are affecting the stock movement. These indicators will often use a standardized price history by establishing the lowest and highest prices within a given time period. After that, they will be measuring the securities position in reference to that range. These indicators will also tell you when a stock is being over or under bought. When a stock is overbought that means it's overdue for a reversal in the trend, as the stock has risen too high. Oversold means the same thing but implies the stock will rise.

While you'll find that many swing traders are looking for the one system of indicators that will always give them the correct result that just doesn't exist. Unfortunately, every indicator can be wrong, swing trading isn't just a concrete science that will always give you profits. If it was everyone would do it, and more importantly, we'd use computer programs for it.

This is why fundamental analysis is so important, it helps you figure out when the technical indicators you're observing are actually correct, rather than simply leaving it to guesswork. You'll find that many swing traders will neglect fundamental analysis even though it is what can help you really get ahead of the market.

2. Compare the Stock to the Rest of the Overall Market- This step, also known as relative strength analysis involves the comparison of the performance of a stock to its market or industry. By looking at the disparity between these two, you'll be able to tell whether or not the stock you've chosen is performing good or bad.

Divergences are extremely good signals because they show you how well the stock of your choice is performing regardless of the way the industry, in particular, is performing.

The Wider View-Fundamental Analysis

If fundamental analysis sounds like a 9-headed hydra to you, and you aren't feeling very much like Heracles, don't be afraid. We'll be using the KISS approach to fundamental analysis in this book. Which is to say we'll "Keep It Simple Stupid."

Now, I'm not going to try to set you up for your MBA in economics. What I'm trying to do here is present you the actually important bits. That is to say that we'll be looking at the most important, key parts of a firm's fundamentals. Only those that affect stock prices are really important to us. After all, we're traders, not economists.

Fundamental analysis is about constantly asking questions. You'll be asking questions like how fast is this company growing, what is its position in relation to the competition, what about the returns?

Through repeatedly answering these questions over and over again, you'll begin to have an idea of what the company's shares should be trading at. Often, you'll find that they aren't trading at that point, which is where you make your entry.

You're not going to find the intrinsic value of a stock that institutions like Wall Street are trying to calculate (the intrinsic value is the true value of the company, rather than simply being the value that the market arrives at.) On the other hand, you don't need the intrinsic value. You're not trying to find the value of the shares down to a singular cent. On the other hand, if you determine their value is between $30 and $50 but they're trading at $20 then you don't need much more to invest.

Getting To Grips with Why It Works

There's much less debate on whether or not fundamental analysis works compared to technical analysis working. After all, the whole field of investing is rooted in it. The more a company earns the more people are willing to pay to have a share of it. Let's say you rent out an apartment for $500 a month, regardless of how much you think the true value of a $500 a month apartment is, it'll be half of the value of a $1000 apartment.

Naturally, fundamental analysis is a bit more complex than this in practice. You'll be looking at quarterly earnings rather than $500 or $1000 a month. The point, however, is that fundamental analysis tries to get the value of a company from its projected future earning potential.

Arbitrageurs are a vital component of why fundamental analysis works. They are generally looking for riskless profits for themselves. For example, if a share is, say $20 a pop, and the firm is valued at $1 billion, then if the firm has $2 billion on their bank, with no debt then an Arbitrageur will pop in and buy a ton of those shares.

The Arbitrageurs taking advantage of such miss-pricings is what helps the market stay afloat. The Arbitrageur might even buy the company for $1 billion and pay for it using the money that the company had on its pricing books.

The bottom line is- fundamental analysis works because entities such as investors, firms or governments pursue riskless profits endlessly.

How to Start Trading

In this chapter, I'll guide you through selecting a quality broker for yourself and opening a trading account. In addition to that, we'll be looking at service providers, starting a trading journal, as well as how to maintain a good mentality to succeed as one.

Brokers

Much like every other kind of trader, swing traders rely on brokers. On the other hand, a swing trader needs to use a different kind of broker from the rest of them. This will depend on a variety of factors we'll be going through in this chapter.

Those factors will be broken down step by step in this chapter, in addition to a variety of details needed to open a brokerage account. After you're done with that, all you need to do is grab a few services to conduct analysis for you.

While some services are useful for conducting market screening, others will chart stocks etc. It's important to decide how much you want to invest in your setup, and I'll recommend some quality services so you can make your pick based on your needs. In addition to this, we'll be making a trading journal, which is, as you'll soon find, one of the most useful tools for a trader out there.

Now, why is the firm that's executing all of your trades being called a broker? It doesn't precisely sound like the best of names and quite frankly sounds much shadier than it should. Brokers really aren't a complicated subject.

Even though their name sounds a bit intimidating, you need a broker in order to become a swing trader…or well, to be a trader in any capacity. On the other hand, due to the wonderful capitalistic market we have, not all brokers are the same. Some will give you highly customized advice while others specialize much more in wealth-management. Some of the highest net-worth people out there participate in these trades. After all, these brokers are quite worth it. Naturally, some of these higher-quality brokers will charge massive fees, because, well, they can simply afford to do it? Generally, they'd tell you that the massive fees they offer are reflective of their advice.

You don't need this. Well, unless you're a billionaire, in which case I think you already know all you need about trading. The brokers that use swing traders use are much lower costed. They are so called no-frill brokers. The good thing about these brokers is that due to competition, even they are giving ATM card access, check-writing privileges etc.

Now, with all of those factors, how do you pick one?

The most common factor I see aspiring traders looking at is commissions. After all, nobody wants a broker to take any sum of their profits. This is a mistake.

Now, now, before you rush me down and put me on a pike, I am not trying to say they don't matter. Naturally, fees do matter. Swing trading wasn't even possible in the olden days due to the massive commissions that were everywhere.

Today, it's different. Fees these days really aren't that much, you'll be paying something like a flat $5-12 per trade that you make, which can easily be less than 0.1%

of your trading volume. The difference between $5 and $12 isn't large to you, however, it might mean that you get some extra perks you otherwise wouldn't.

Now, some of the other factors are:

- *Charting systems- If you rely a lot on technical analysis when you're making your trades then you'll be wanting a broker that's good at charting. The charting quality and ease of reading can make the difference between success and failure.*
- *Customer service- In my opinion, this is the single most important factor to look at when selecting a broker. Keep in mind these are people that will be handling massive amounts of your money. You don't want to put it in the hands of someone who you can't properly reach when you need them. Every trader will also sometimes run into problems with their broker, and in those times, this really counts.*

- *Ease of Deposits and Withdrawals- How easy it is to get money from your broker is only important when you're trading for a living. If it's hard, you won't have an easy time getting that monthly paycheck. On the* other hand deposits are very important when making time-sensitive trades.

Which brokers you're going to choose also depends on how much you're planning to spend, fundamentally, there are two kinds of brokers:

1. Discount Brokers: These brokers are those that instead of offering quality and high-tier services, simply focus on executing trades. You tell them what you want bought and sold, they do that. Naturally, most of these trades will be made through the PC, unless you pay extra for phone support. These brokers are generally cheaper, and offer fewer services.

2. Direct access firms- Direct access firms are those companies that let you go past a broker and trade with an exchange or market without a middleman. The advantage of doing this is that you'll have way more control due to being able to see who's offering what and for how much.

Usually, these brokers will require you to get some software that will give you very high-speed data, usually superior to streaming sites. While some discount brokers are offering direct access trading, these are generally worse at it than dedicated companies.

2.5 Full Service Brokers- This isn't really on the list because it's not for you. These are brokers like Merrill Lynch, they will offer you a bazillion different services, and charge you just about as much. A swing trader shouldn't need anyone whispering down their ear about what trades to make. Swing trading is a road of independence, you don't need someone else telling you what trades to take and what trades you shouldn't take.

I'm not going to recommend a single broker to you in this book, after all, the quality of brokers easily changes over time. Because of that, I can't really tell you which brokers are good or bad. On the other hand, I also can't know which country you're in, and while most of this book is US-driven, the fundamentals I want to apply everywhere. Just keep in mind to select quality brokers that offer everything you need!

You Need Some Standards Girl

Now, much like a girl that's just entered college, and is faced with the abundance of guys hitting on her, you'll need some standards to pick up the diamonds from the rough.

So, let me give you some baseline things to look for in a broker, like an older girl in a sorority.

Commissions: Never overpay, anything above $10 flat is a bit of a rip-off - that also shouldn't be more than 1-2c off of every share you're buying. Anything higher than this is pretty much just the broker preying on new people like you. It's also important to note that the higher your fees are, the more money you need to earn before you break even. While I've recommended some specific rates just now, too many people look only at rates and nothing else. That is the biggest noob trap in the whole world of trading, and there are a lot of noob traps. Commission rates are important but not as important as some other things.

Versatility: In this day and age, it's very important for your broker to offer to trade more securities than just stocks. Naturally, while most of us start off at stocks, trading other markets is also very popular. If your broker can figure out how to get you trading international securities, currencies etc. then that's a big plus. Naturally, you should be expecting to pay a small premium on top of the standard fee for services like this.

Various Banking Services: You'll find that some brokers are willing to give you services like check-writing or ATM transactions. These are generally just hassle-free measures to get your money. If you aren't trading seriously I'd recommend fetching one of these. With that being said, pretty much every broker will let you get your stuff to your PayPal card, so it shouldn't be all that hard getting your money.

Usability: This refers to your broker's UI and is possibly one of the most important thing about a broker. Think about it like looks in a guy, while they may not be the most important thing, everyone has a baseline of what they'll accept, and if he's pretty enough, most other things won't matter. Well, similarly to that, don't forget to check under the hood of the pretty ones, as they often don't contain everything else you need. On the other hand, a user-friendly and usable UI can make trading much easier, or even increase your profits. If it's quick and easy to place orders you're much less likely to get stressed out and make a bad trade or several. Also note that some brokers will let you test out a demo version of their platform before signing up.

Varied Amenities: Amenities are things that include services conductive to research and charting services. Let's give you an example, a discount broker may be willing to give you level 2 quotes- these will give you the access to order books for Nasdaq stocks. You will also get stock reports from Wall Street, as well as other research reports. On the other hand, these aren't really useful when swing trading due to the short-term nature of it.

Customer Service: This is the one thing I can't stress enough. It's the equivalent of a guy's core values. Sure, you can make do without them for a time, but after some time, you'll find that you're simply incompatible and nothing else can make up for them. It's very hard to determine how responsive a broker will be unless you rely on the internet, so check reviews and do a detailed analysis of every one of them when it comes to customer service. You want to be able to get your broker on the phone whenever you need them, rather than waiting for when it may be too late.

Reports and Analysis: This is the part of a broker that determines how well they can present you your data. Do they provide you year-to-date portfolio index returns? While sure, you could calculate this all yourself, having a broker do it is much easier. It's also great to have tax services in countries that have manual tax reports like the US.

The First Step-Opening an Account

After you've made your pick as to which broker you want to do business with, you'll need to decide on the kind of account you want to open with them.

Here you've got a variety of options, based on whether borrowing money to trade from your broker sounds appealing, as well as your position on trading futures or placing the account on your name or your spouse. You can even make the account a retirement account, or a traditional investing account. The next two questions will answer this, well except the spouse one, that one's to be had between the two of you...I'm not good at relationship counseling.

Cash or Margin Account

Whether you want to get a cash or margin account will depend on you after selecting, which broker you, want to do business with. When you get this choice, keep in mind that cash restricts you to trading with funds you have available, while margin accounts allow you to borrow from your broker to trade. Picking an account is also necessary if you want trading options.

A swing trader with say, $30 000 can borrow up to $30 000 usually, now, this is a double edged sword. Let's say you invest all of it...and you lose 10%, instead of losing

3000 you'll be losing 6000 due to the money you borrowed. Margin accounts tend to make traders much more reckless. By being allowed to trade with money that isn't really yours the dealership is trying to get you to pay a fee on the money you borrowed. These can easily lead to you getting in way over your head.

If you're a new trader (as you probably are) you should be sticking exclusively to cash accounts.

Traditional vs Retirement Account

The second account division is traditional and retirement. The difference is really quite self-explanatory.

Now, the biggest difference here is well, taxes. Traditional accounts will let you take your money whenever you want, and however much of it you want to take out. On the other hand, they also mean that you have to report this as taxable income. In the US at least, if you get classified as a full time trader you can make less taxes by turning these gains from capital to ordinary. This is important because if you aren't classified as a full time trader then you're going to have to pay the full capital tax.

A retirement account stops these problems, however, the government doesn't like this idea, and hence stops you from putting as much money as you'd like into it. Your IRA caps out at $5000 a year if you're under 49. The government also limits you when it comes to taking that money out, in most countries you can only do it after turning 59.

These kinds of inconveniences tend to be why people elect to not open a retirement account. If you just want to max out your retirement, then opening a retirement account is definitely the best idea.

Picking a Service Provider

Unfortunately, trading without a service provider is pretty much impossible. On the other hand, these are all different from each other, so a newbie might get overwhelmed by choice when selecting them.

These differ in a few ways but mainly its timelines, quality, and breadth of data that makes the final decision. What you want in one of these is all the services that you need. Primarily, you'll want charting and access to a database. You'll need those to conduct both technical and fundamental analysis. Now we're going to go over the main things you'll want to look for in a service provider.

Now, let's sit down and take a short lesson on the service provider business model first. They make money by making a deal with a data provider, and then providing you with the data that is relevant for you.

Service providers will be giving you the tools to find and chart the stocks that you want, which will increase the amount of info you have on the market. Using tools such as these is flexible enough to let you change all of your inputs. Ranging from what indicators to use to which criteria to pay attention to.

Providers are classified into two main categories. You've probably guessed it, it's those that provide technical data, and those that provide fundamental data. Those that provide both are therefore classed as unicorns.

A strong charting system is, well, pretty much necessary if you want to be a successful swing trader. They simply do way too much for you to be successful without them. That isn't to say it's straight-up impossible, but it will be far more difficult compared to just taking a provider and going with it.

You will absolutely require real time charts and quotes. Real time here means that they are of live market data, and are not being delayed by an external cause. If your plans are to trade interday, then when you enter your orders, you don't really need real time charting. After all, you'll be entering orders after-market hours. The market has a ludicrous amount of charting providers, and most of these cater to the active traders that are in their system. This is to say that most discount brokers will have connections with some charting systems. In fact, order entry is often integrated with charting, allowing you to make automatic buys and sells, which is a great feature.

While there are a lot of excellent charting services online, I can't really recommend any off the tip of the hat, because I don't know what country you're in and what the rules there might be. With that being said, I would check it out online and then determine if you need additional charting.

Now, charting systems themselves can be difficult to select from. After all, every provider will try to make themselves look different. Spoiler alert: Most of them aren't all that different. All you need to do is pay attention to what you need, the primary concern will be ease of use. After all, you won't have all day to fish out charts, you need them to be available pretty much at the snap of your fingers. Consider their visual appeal and clarity as well, you don't want to spend hours on just reading a chart.

Features such as being able to input your own indicators are excellent for advanced traders. If your plan is to stick with a single one for all of your career, then try to look for one that lets you insert custom indicators. You'll be thanking me later.

When it comes to selecting these programs I recommend checking the rankings made by Technical Analysis of Stocks & Commodities in its yearly Reader's Choice Awards. I use two charting systems: one, which is specially provided by my broker and another one in which I make the bulk of my personal research.

Fundamental analysis software lets traders who decide upon using fundamental analysis in investing as a process need to get a subscription to data providers that can assist them in their research.

It's lucky that most of a company's fundamental data, ranging from historical earnings to expected growth, is available... for free... online, God bless the internet. Honestly, it's amazing how far trading has come, and how easy it is to come across this stuff online these days.

Like seriously, just open Google Finance and look at all it gives you. Ten years ago, my broker couldn't have given me that much information. And this is all FREE, in this age of digitalization, it's important to remember that most of the things you need are available online, if you know how to look for it.

Let's look at, say, Yahoo! Finance (God that's a name I haven't heard in a long time.)

The site will give you:

- Rudimentary charts to help out your trades
- Headlines which the stock of your choice has made in recent days
- The company profile of the owner company of your stock
- The information on the company's main competitors
- The estimates of other analysts as to where the value will go
- The companies income statement

- The balance sheet of the company you're looking at

This and many other things are all available for free. Beware, though, that it does have a message board. Run away from those, for reasons we'll discuss soon, you don't want to be getting into any message boards just yet (or, well, ever really.)

Reuters is another site you can use. While sites like Yahoo! and Google will give you aggregate data, Reuters makes its own data. The main categories available on the website are Stock Overview, Financial Highlights, Estimates, Officers and Directors, Financial Statements, Recommendations, and Analyst Research. All of these have some of their uses, though as a swing trader you'll be primarily looking at Ratios.

The excellent thing about this site is the variety of data it provides. It will give you data on a company vs its peers as well as other things. Such as whether the company is going through good or bad times, as well as free research services. On the other hand, the paid subs are also quite great.

Fundamental Analysis

When you are trying to find the best stock to take on, you want to focus on different analyses which will help you make an informed decision. One of these types of analysis is fundamental analysis. Fundamental analysis is performed when you are doing general research on a company. For example, if you are interested in purchasing Amazon stock, you will start to look into the company. You might start with the company's history to get a sense of the overall growth of the entity itself. You might decide that looking over the last few years will give you enough history to help you make an informed decision. While how much research you do is more of your personal preference and how serious you take your career as a trader, I believe that the more information you have on a company, the better chance you have of becoming successful.

Fundamental Variables

There are going to be several questions that come to your mind immediately as you start to perform research on a company. For example, you might ask yourself how long the company has been successful. You might ask yourself if this is a company you believe will give you a good profit or if this company has a history of getting traders high returns. Whatever questions you ask yourself, you need to realize that you have to do more than just ask the basic questions. In fact, you have to make sure you take time to look at the fundamental variables.

Positive Earnings Adjustment

In the trading world, there are people who are known as market analysts. These are people who will often analyze how well companies are doing and then give the companies a review or a forecast, which allows other people to notice where the company is sitting. Market reviewers are typically known as cautious people and don't tend to believe that companies will pass their forecast. However, this does happen and when it does, it brings us into positive earnings adjustment.

Basically, this states that we need to look for stocks which have surprised the market analysts. This is because if companies pass their forecast, they will continue to succeed. Therefore, they become known as one of the best companies to gain a profit from, which is always a great thing for a trader to know. However, you will still want to make sure that you do your deep analysis before making any moves on a stock.

Positive Earning Revision

This is the process that market analysts go through when they are evaluating how well a company is doing so they can give them a forecast. As stated above, these analysts are cautious and very careful to note where they think the company is going. Therefore, when the company goes farther than what they initially thought, they need to re-evaluate the company. Of course, admitting they are wrong is not an easy thing for analysts to do as it isn't easy for anyone. However, when they do need to admit this, people can quickly learn what companies they should start paying attention to.

Earnings Momentum

While there are many important fundamental variables to look at when you are making an analysis, earnings momentum holds a special place. This variable is very important, especially when it comes to bull markets. Earnings momentum is the variable which looks at the year to year growth of earnings. Therefore, this is what will often set the price for stocks.

Strong Cash Flow

This is another fundamental variable that will tell you how much free cash a company has. This is a very important variable because it will let you know where a company financially sits after it has paid all of its bills and expenses. When you are getting into trading, you want to pay attention to the companies who are financially stable. You want to make sure that a company can grow because the more they grow, the more profit that you can make. Think about it – if you put your money into a stock where the company could barely pay the electric bill, do you think that your money would be secure, if even for a period of time? You want to make place your money in companies which are financially secure.

Earnings Growth

Another variable you want to pay attention to is how much more money the company is making as the years go on. When you look at this variable, you will be looking at the earnings growth variable. This is another company that you would think of investing in because you know that they have seen considerable growth for a certain number of years. Therefore, you analyze that the company will only continue to grow.

Technical Analysis

Technical analysis is as important as fundamental analysis, especially when it comes to swing trading. However, you could view technical analysis as the more serious of the two types of analysis. Instead of just looking at the basics of the company and the fundamental variables which focus on your potential stock's company, you will focus more on the technical side of your stock when you look at technical analysis.

By definition, technical analysis is measuring the historical trends of the stock. Because many people feel that technical analysis is trickier than fundamental analysis, it might be wise to do more research about the topic before you start analyzing any stocks. There are a few online classes and books that are available for you, if you feel the need to become well educated on technical analysis.

One of the biggest factors to remember when you are focusing on technical analysis is you want to make sure to study every detail of your stock's history. You want to make sure you understand the trend, have made any notes you needed to, and that you believe you see the trend giving you the best profit before you decide to take on the stock. Technical analysis is going to take time and patience. However, you also don't want to spend too much time trying to decide if you want to take on a specific stock or not. This is a special time balance that you will figure out once have opened your account and on your way to trading stocks.

What You Will Study Through Technical Analysis

There are several details of the stock's history that you will look at when you are focusing on the technical analysis part of your trading schedule. This is something that you will do with every stock as it will help you decide if this stock is going to be worth your energy and time.

In order to give you a better view of what type of things you will look for, I will briefly discuss them below.

Study of Charts

Of course, one of the main pieces of the stock you will look at are the historical charts. These charts will give you some of the most detailed information that will help you make the best decision possible for your swing trading journey.

One of the most common charts are known as candlestick charts. These charts received this name because they are shaped like a candlestick. On top of that, the information you will find in the chart is designed through the candlestick. There are two main reasons why traders like candlestick charts so much. First, these charts are fairly easy to read and understand. Not only do they give you the information you need to know but they will also show off colors. The second reason is because these charts are known to give you an indication that the trend is about to change. For many people, this is extremely helpful because it decreases the amount of research that you need to do. However, there are other people that still say you should always perform your own research to make sure that the candlestick chart is correct on its assumption.

In general, the candlestick chart will tell you what the opening price was for the stock, the highest price, the lowest price, and the closing price. By getting these prices, you will start to analyze the chart to see what type of trend this stock is following. By looking at the history of the stock, you can start to get a sense of what the average prices are throughout the day. On top of this, you will also be able to get a sense of how much the stock tends to jump up and down during the day. On top of this, the candlestick chart will change colors in the center, depending on if the stock made a profit that day between the opening and closing price.

Of course, you will want to do this type of analysis for any chart that you come across, whether it is a line or pie chart. While each chart will look a bit different, they will all have the same valuable information within them. They will all tell you what the prices were throughout the day. However, not all of the charts will give you a prediction to what the trend will be doing next.

Volume

Another major part of technical analysis is the volume of a stock. The reasons why the volume is so important is because you will be able to get a sense of the intensity of the stock's movement in price. What this means is you will be able to take a certain amount of time, whether it is a few hours or a few months and get an idea of how many shares were traded during this time. Of course, the more shares that you find are traded, the better the stock is for trading. Stocks tend to reach high volume for many reasons. For example, they could be considered one of the more popular trading stocks on the market, such as Apple or Target. Another reason is because higher volume tends to mean a better profit. Think about it –

people don't often take on trades where they are less likely to make a profit. Therefore, if the volume is high you know that most traders have found this stock to be successful.

Analyzing the Trend Line

I have already discussed a lot of information about trend lines in this book. By now, you should know that it is one of the main factors that will help you determine the success rate of a stock and whether you want to take on this stock or not. However, I feel it is important to mention that whenever you are analyzing a trend line, you are using technical analysis. You are not only analyzing what the trend line has done the previous day or the last couple of days, but you are most likely looking at the trend line over a period of months. The farther back you go, the more you will be able to learn details about the stock's trends.

Watch for Counter Trends

A counter trend is an opposing move that is a part of an overall, larger trend in one direction. For example, a stock of successful and growing tech company is going to spend a lot of time moving upward. As part of that larger upward trend, there will be counter-trends that temporarily move in the opposite direction. Counter trends can represent buying opportunities.

ABCD Patterns

The so-called A-B-C-D chart pattern indicates a breakout to higher price levels. The stock rises to an initial high at point A, which is followed by a counter-trend to point B. The price level A represents the 'breakout' price that the trader expects to either represent the high price point or a coming marker for higher prices. The point B is taken as the risk level or new level of support. After reaching point B, the stock will rise a little and show a slower uptrend along C, until it eventually reaches a new high at D. The trader will use point A as the guideline that can determine where to set a limit order to sell and take profits.

Trading Volume

Trading volume is an important indicator, as we mentioned earlier. One of the first things you will need to do when considering volume is to determine what the historical trading volume for a stock is. The word historical should be considered carefully, as historical doesn't necessarily mean you take the all-time average or go back 20 years ago. Historical trading volume that is more relevant is how it has been going recently. If you start to see a large increase in trading volume coupled with a trend reversal that could be a signal that more trend reversal is coming. Whenever you see other signals, such as candlestick indicators that are coupled with increased volume that should reinforce your confidence in a trading situation.

Retracements vs. Reversals

One of the most important things that new swing traders need to become conscious of are retracements. These are small counter trends that can look like trend reversals over the short term, but they are not real reversals. Rather, they are small random blips in the midst of a solid trend that is continuing one direction or the other. They key to recognizing a retracement as compared to a genuine reversal, and its not easy, is to look for the share price breaking through previous levels of support if we are looking for a new downward trend, or resistance if we are looking to identify a new upward trend. This chart showing SPY, which tracks the S & P 500, is a good example. For most of 2018 SPY showed a steady upward trend. Retracements are indicated by the dotted arrows. These were short term counter trends that were not interrupting the inexorable upward trend. Toward the end of the year, we see a massive downshift that broke levels of support. That is indicated by the dotted oval in the chart. This was followed by a genuine downward trend. Note the rise in trading volume indicated by the vertical bars at the bottom of the chart.

You will notice that another signal is present toward the right side of the chart. While SPY seemed to enter a sideways area for a time, there is another red candle with an extremely large body, which of course was followed by plummeting share prices.

Even professional traders have difficulty distinguishing between a retracement and a real change in trend that would qualify as a reversal, but you should spend time studying charts so that you can begin to recognize retracements more often than not.

Pin bars and price rejection

One thing to look for at (what may be) the peak of upward trends or (what may be) the bottom of a downward trend is a pin bar. This is a narrow bodied candlestick with a long wick sticking out in one direction or the other. When a candlestick has a long wick that means either the low or high price was way out of proportion to the open and closing prices – and so was rejected. A high price that is rejected at the top of an upturn can indicate a coming reversal. In the snapshot below, the green or bullish candle in the middle has a high price that went well above the closing price, and you can see this was followed by two bearish candlesticks (two days of declining prices). This could be taken as a sell signal, or a buy signal if you were shorting the stock.

At the bottom of an uptrend, when you see a low price that was rejected, that is the candle ended up with a much higher closing price, it could be a buy signal for bullish investors. Of course, you should always protect yourself by utilizing a stop loss order. In the event that you are wrong, you can put the stop loss order at slightly below the most recent low, to prevent your trade from being caught up in a renewed downward trend.

Inside Bars

Another price action strategy is to look for inside bars. This is when a long bar is followed by a smaller bar that would completely fit inside the previous bar, but it's the opposite type. So its kind of like the reverse of an engulfing patter. Forex traders in particular like trading inside bars. They can represent a coming breakout.

In the image above, on the left we have a bullish bar followed by a smaller bearish candlestick, while on the right side we see the opposite situation, a bearish bar followed by a smaller bullish bar. If either of these are seen in part of a trending market, they can be taken as a signal of a coming breakout. When occurring in or near a level of support or resistance, the pattern can indicate a coming trend reversal. You should confirm this type of signal with other indicators.

Breakout & Breakdown trading

Break out trading and breakdown trading is typically what most traders look to trade when starting out. With this type of trading, one needs to be super disciplined in the approach you are taking. Having exact breakout and breakdown levels so you know when you need to get out of the trade and stops even if the stop is a mental one will keep you on the profitable side of trading. With this type of trading, taking quick profits is the name of the game and going in with a larger than average size will help the profits add up quickly. Although most beginners look to this type of trading starting out, most if not all traders eventually blow up accounts trading this strategy for a very simple reason: No discipline. This type of trading can be very profitable if the discipline is there. Having the exact entry and exit points are key in determining if you are going to be a profitable trader. This strategy typically works best if you have done your homework and are comfortable with the subject of support and resistance areas and are quick in reading the chart in determining which way the stock is going. Being reactionary works best with this trading style, let the area of support or resistance break before you buy or sell short and immediately have an area in which you get out to protect your account. Typically, if a breakout does not work you will know immediately. A few steps to help you stay on the right side of the trade

Step 1 – Identify why you think the stock/ticker will break out (Find the catalyst).

Step 2 – Draw support and resistance areas on the chart (Premarket information should be enabled on your platform).

Step 3 – Determine which way the stock/ticker is trending. If trending up you are looking at a previous area on the chart for resistance to break and a series of higher lows and higher highs into that break out point. The more times the breakout area is reached and not broken the better, the follow through on the trade once the area has broken will be more substantial. If trending down you are looking at a support area to break and a series of lower lows and lower highs into that break point. The same thing applies here as well in terms of how many times the support area is touched but not broken.

Step 4 – Identify your stop points for the trade. This is one of the most important steps here. Not identifying your stop points will ensure your trading career is short. Having a plan when trading is crucial towards your profitability as a trader and will give you the discipline needed to succeed. No plan, no success – simple as that.

Step 5 – Once you have identified the general direction of the stock/ticker, figured out your stop points next it is time to decide the position size of the trade based on how much you are willing to risk.

Step 6 – After all these things have been identified, next is to enter the trade based on the trend of the stock.

I know it may seem like a lot of things you have to consider before you enter a trade, this is to make sure that you enter the trade with an entry plan as well as an exit plan to protect your account in case there is the breakout fails to follow through.

Now that we went over the reasons for getting into a trade and how to judge and what to do when getting into a trade, let's go over the specific things when looking for breakouts and breakdowns.

Breakouts

When I am trading breakouts I am looking for specific types of resistance levels here. The resistance levels that I am looking for are levels that have been tested more than once and seen some significant retrace of the current up move. Once that level has been tested a few times I follow the steps above to determine where I need to get in and how much I am willing to risk based on the stop area. See the Chart below – KONE as of 7/21/2016.

Breakdowns

Some of my favorite trades here, when trading breakdowns the move typically happens quickly because of human psychology. Fear is a stronger emotion than greed, so when you are trading to the downside you need to be extremely disciplined because if the breakdown doesn't happen the ticker will turn around almost immediately and you'll be down 25 or 30 cents within a second. Identifying your stop out area first here is crucial. When the support area is identified, take a step back and look at the overall trend to make sure you see the pattern that you are seeing instead of an intermediate low in an uptrend, which is what newbie traders tend to do and have large losses in trading the downside. Trading the downside is harder than trading the upside or breakout. To be on the safe side let the support area break here and then let it retest the area and continue in the downtrend you were anticipating. See the example below.

In the above chart you can see the areas that you need to pay attention to when trading to the downside. You see the first highs around the $4.70s range this is the initial high here. Then the low was put in and the previous high was broken. The low area is where a lot of traders tend to get trapped thinking that it's off its highs it needs to go back down. This is what we call consolidation. The smart money is taking profits and churning individuals in and out of the stock while getting ready for the next leg up. Typically if you are looking at the 1 minute chart there is some confusion on this time frame, try looking at the 5 minute to see what is going on there this will typically give you a better idea of what the stock/ticker is currently doing. Churning individuals in and out of the stock is not an uncommon thing. The smart money is trying to get everyone going in the same direction before pushing it the other way, this also holds for breakouts as well. The lower high here is the confirmation of the trend that you are looking for to the downside. This is the type of picture perfect high, low, lower high you are looking for. If you look at the chart you can see a huge resistance area that kept pushing the stock/ticker down and the support area that needed to break was the New Low identified on the chart or the lower low. Once you have the lower high and the lower low breaks you are in a confirmed downtrend and you can hold the trade. The area we identified as the entry point was on the lower high, out stop was tight here and we know what we were looking for in terms of the actual break here. The reason I identified this area as entry is because of the resistance area right above and how the stock/ticker backed off every single time. The entry that you should take would be the break of the "New Low" identified on the chart.

Trading is one of the most difficult things that I have undertaken, but it has also been the most rewarding. There is an enormous amount of freedom when trading, you get the feeling that you are on top of the world. Trading can bring you tons of great opportunities to see more things in life and to participate in what is really happening in the market. Your financial IQ will definitely increase because of the amount of detail that is needed to trade successfully. Although this may seem like a hard thing to do, I definitely think anyone with the discipline to follow directions and their own rules can make it trading. The 90% individuals that do not make it trading do not follow rules, do not have a set of rules to follow and are extremely undisciplined traders. The most important part of trading is to understand that losses are just the cost of doing business and they will happen. The successful trader knows this and welcomes small losses in search of the large gains. The best thing to do in trading is to continue to learn, take small losses so you are protecting your principal which will give you more time in the market and give you the opportunity to take advantage of the big trades that will increase your account along the way.

If you have any questions, feel free to email me at *traderjasper@gmail.com*.

Predicting the Market

Indicators and charts are one of the most important components when we talk about technical analysis. In addition to experience, coldness, and psychology, a good analyst cannot disregard a thorough knowledge of the graphs. The latter can represent different information and may appear in different forms.

In graphical analysis, the graphs deserve particular attention because they represent the price dynamics of a given financial instrument and in a given period.

In the technical analysis, the most commonly used type of graph is certainly the candlestick chart, better known under the name of a Japanese candlestick chart. Before moving on to a detailed description of the candlestick chart, however, I would like to say a few words about two other charts, less used than candlestick charts, but which may be useful as they can help you understand the Japanese candlestick chart.

The price chart is shown on a Cartesian plane where, on the abscissa axis, that is the vertical axis the time is reported, while on the horizontal axis the price is reported.

Given this premise, we can still say that the graphs refer to different time periods whether they are fractions of minutes, hours and days, if not even weeks, months or even years indicating different sizes of opening or closing, of maximums and minima.

On the axis of the abscissas, we find a space called histogram of the volume, which represents the quantity of instruments exchanged during the period under examination.

In graphic analysis in the specific and more generally in the technical analysis, various types of graph are used.

Features of a good chart

With the above, I do not mean that you will need a chart that contains a myriad of information or detailed information in detail, but I would like to emphasize that the best successful traders on the market, use very few indicators. Yes, you understood correctly. Only a few indicators. You will, therefore, think that what has been described up to now is only a chat, but it is not so, as these extrapolate the most important information directly from the graph. The charts obviously can only be provided by the brokers, which as for the forex market, here too we advise you always to choose the best binary options brokers. So it is not true that the graphics are all the same, it will be the good broker to extrapolate all the information that interests him from the various detailed charts. And from here we recognize the best brokers.

The reason for this extrapolation is very simple: since the indicators express only the past in a graphic form, they can provide a very approximate vision of the future. So too many indicators in a chart can sometimes create confusion instead of aid.

Therefore, we consider it very important to keep the following points in mind:

    1. Good graphic program.

With this, in fact, you should always be able to look far enough in the past, to plan the future and identify relevant barriers and gather a satisfactory overview. In the binary options charts of the different brokers, this time frame is too narrow to draw reliable conclusions.

    1. Good quality graphs always indicate different time intervals.

These range from a few minutes to a max. of a month.

    1. Never set just a common linear chart.

This fact would not be very useful for technical analysis purposes. On the other hand, candle or beam charts are used, which we will explain briefly.

What is chart analysis?

The analysis of the graphs is above all the search for particular shapes, also called graphic structures, configurations, figures.

They are figures that emerge from the price movement, and that can signal its future trend. They are tracked by analysts joining points in the price graph of a financial security or the performance of an indicator.

The purpose of the graphic analysis will, therefore, be to identify the most typical price patterns for forecasting purposes.

These graphic formations can be classified into different categories. The main categories of classes can assume inversion or continuation or consolidation characteristics. Fundamental feature will also be the dynamics of the volumes, which we will explain under each figure.

This is why it takes technique, experience, strategies, if not the analyst's ability to see these forms in the movement of a graph. These are the fundamental elements of this type of analysis. The concept of trendline, support and resistance are also part of this aspect of technical analysis.

Below we will list the most used graphs for graphic analysis and explain the operation. Before doing this, however, we must explain another very important and used concept: the figure of Continuation. These have common characteristics in all the graphs, they represent a pause in the prevailing trend in progress and are a prelude to a continuation of the trend in the direction of the direction previously underway. For this reason, they are also known as consolidation figures.

The main difference between the continuation and the inversion figures concerns the extension.

The continuation figures are often accompanied by a decrease in the volumes traded.

One of the first figures we are going to examine is the wedge.

Wedge

This too is a continuation figure on explained and is very similar to the triangle for 2 reasons:

- for the form;
- for the time it takes to form. This differs from the triangle that we will see below because the shape that forms is characterized by a strongly bullish or bearish inclination opposite to that of the current trend.

This means that:

this chart consists of two convergent trend lines and takes about one to three months to develop;

in an uptrend, a falling wedge or "a descending wedge" can be encountered;

while in a bearish tendency a rising wedge or "an ascending wedge" can develop.

As with the pennant and flag figures, the wedge can be found in the middle of a movement, thus allowing to calculate minimum targets.

The dynamics of the volumes see a decrease in the course of the formation of the pattern and it should go to be reduced for all the period of formation of the figure. On the contrary, they increase significantly when the trend line is broken, which is a typical feature of the wedge.

Pennant

This figure is also quite common in chart analysis.

This figure together with the figure of the flag, which we will see immediately after the flag appears after an almost vertical movement and represents a pause in the trend.

Its characteristic is that it is presented as a symmetrical triangle which, however, has a maximum extension of 3 weeks. Most often, in bearish actions, the refinement time of the figure is even lower and is equal to one or maximum two weeks. The pennant is halfway to the bullish or bearish movement, with the obvious implications in calculating the minimum targets for the movement's arrival.

It will, therefore, be obvious that the volume decreases during the formation of the figure and should be low throughout the period of formation of the pattern. On the contrary, instead, they increase significantly when the trendline breaks, which identifies the pennant. These are accompanied by a similar trend in the range within which prices move.

Pennants, most often coincide with a contraction phase, which does not necessarily have an opposite inclination with respect to the basic trend.

Both this figure and the next develop within a rather short time frame.

The third figure that we examine as announced is the Flag.

Flag

Flag formation, or flag, is a very common pattern of continuation in graphic analysis.

This form tends to appear close to the temporary exhaustion of a trend, which represents a brief pause in the market after strongly accentuated movements, are almost vertical and known as flagpole.

The flag has a shape similar to a parallelepiped, almost to represent a rectangle, bounded by two parallel trendlines but opposed to the prevailing trend.

in other words, it can be seen as a flag that is tilted downward in an uptrend and upward in a bearish trend.

His training ends within a medium period, that is between one and three weeks. It usually appears halfway to complete movement.

It must also be said that if it is in a bearish movement the perfection time is less and the figure is usually completed in one or two weeks. Precisely because it is in the middle of the bullish or bearish movement, the figure is important for identifying price targets. From here we will then calculate the width of the movement preceding the flag and report this distance after the break of the trend line delineating the figure.

The volume should also decrease during the formation of the figure and then increase again when the trend line is broken.

So let's see how to use Flag and Pennant.

The targets that can be identified in relation to these figures are two:

- The first is determined by projecting the width of the base from the breakout point; here this target assumes less importance if we consider the reduced dimensions of the figure.

- The second can instead be obtained by projecting, from the breakout point, a distance equivalent to that covered by the movement that preceded the formation of the pennant.
- This means that these figures often materialize around half of the overall movement, giving a fair advantage at the operational level.

The temporary phase of price weakness can be exploited to enter the stock or even just to increase the position taken earlier, again using a stop-loss much lower than the potential take-profit.

The rectangle will represent the fourth figure that we will explain.

Rectangle

The rectangle is the simplest among the figures proposed by the technical analysis.

It identifies a phase of price congestion. In Technical Analysis, with this term, we mean a graphic formation in correspondence with which prices oscillate within a narrow range of values. This process takes place when the market moves sideways.

The pattern represents a break zone of the current trend in which prices move sideways. This also gives rise to the name of trading range or congestion area, a figure that represents a period of consolidation of the current trend that is resolved in the direction of the trend that preceded it. This represents a fundamental figure, to correctly identify the continuation pattern if not also the observation of the volumes.

Also, for this bullish figure, the rebounds must be accompanied by high volumes, with the corrections characterized by decreasing volumes. In the opposite case, instead, in the bearish rectangle, are the corrections to have more accentuated volumes.

Many investors, take advantage of the oscillations, selling to the top of the figure and buying at the minimum. However, those who use this approach risk not exploiting the breaking of the pattern.

The figure in question usually takes from one to three months to improve, and the minimum target is represented by the translation of the height of the rectangle when the price breaks the figure.

Prices move within a fixed band identified by a support and resistance as better shown in the figure below.

first target 1

The rectangles can also be configured as inversion figures, depending on the context in which they are formed. It is therefore evident how the congestion phases identify a moment in which the market expresses considerable uncertainty and awaits new information to decide the future trend. Unlike the contraction phases (in which the continuous reduction in volatility identifies in an increasingly precise manner the moment in which the market will receive the information that awaits) a figure of congestion like the rectangle does not allow to identify sufficiently in advance the moment in which the breakout will take place.

The operational cues that this figure can provide are basically of two types:

- The first requires waiting for the exit of prices from the congestion zone initially identified. This exit must necessarily be classified as a breakout and therefore must be characterized by an increase in volumes and volatility.
- The second operational step derives from the possibility of exploiting the lateral movement of prices to buy close to the identified support and

sell when the values are near the top of the figure again.

Support and Resistance

Let me now explain briefly what are the supports and the resistance.

Support is defined as that price level at which there is, an arrest of the downward trend in prices. An excessive concentration of purchases that occurs in the vicinity of the same will cause a block in the downward trend in prices.

A level of support is defined as reliable when it shows resistance to repeated "attacks" without a bearish breakdown.

The Resistance is defined instead as that level of price where the growth of the same stops. In the case of the Resistance, the high concentration of sales prevents the continuation of the increase.

A resistance level, on the contrary, is stronger and more reliable as it resists repeated "attacks" without an upward failure.

Surely a historical minimum or maximum represents a level of Support or Strategic Resistance.

Consequently, the penetration or breaking of support levels or even resistance can be caused by:

- important changes in the fundamental values of a company (increase in profits, changes in management, etc.);
- from simple forecasts based on price trends in recent times;
- both, both levels of support and resistance can also arise from motivations exclusively of an emotional nature. Supports and resistances represent with great simplicity the encounter/clash between supply and demand.

From the above it is clear that in practice, a breakout, or an event in which the price comes out of a trend, breaking a support or resistance or a channel, above a level of resistance evidence an increase in demand, arising from more buyers, who are willing to buy at higher prices than the current ones.

In the opposite case, instead, the breakdown of a support shows an increase in the sellers, and therefore in the offer, as more sellers are willing to sell even at lower prices than the current ones.

If a level of support is broken, it automatically turns into a resistance level, just as if a resistance level is broken, it becomes a level of support. This process is known as pullback, which is a time when a trending market takes a break.

The support and resistance lines can be drawn horizontally and then we will talk about static support, where the support corresponds to a precise and constant point in time; both obliquely and in this case, we will talk about dynamic support, where a trend line is drawn with the variation of prices and with the passage of time.

The fifth figure, object of study concerns the triangle.

Triangle

In technical analysis, that of the triangle is a consolidation figure and is used to verify the continuation of the main trend. This is a pattern that lasts a few months when there is a pause in the current trend with prices that oscillate in an increasingly narrow area.

The figure has the following characteristics:

The triangle must have a minimum of four reaction points; two superiors, and two inferior; the first ones necessary to trace the upper trend line, the seconds necessary to draw the lower trend line.

A time limit for its resolution characterizes the triangle. Usually, the prices break the triangle at a point between two thirds and three quarters of the depth of the triangle.

The volumes in the formation phase of the triangle waves, lose strength and then explode when the trend line that delimits the figure breaks.

The minimum target for price trends is calculated by projecting the maximum height of the triangle.

The figure in question can present itself according to three different structures:

symmetrical triangle which has the trend lines that delimit it that are convergent.

Prices tend to move in a range that gradually becomes narrower with the passing of the sessions, due to a constant reduction of the maximums, and also due to a constant reduction of the minimums.

descending triangle characterized by a flat demarcation line, the lower one, and by a bearish trend line, the upper one.

In this figure, there will be a greater conviction on the part of the bearish and is often found during a downward trend.

The reduction in the range within which prices move, occurs only thanks to an increase in the minimum, while the maximums remain almost unchanged.

Just such behavior makes evident the greater pressure of the buyers with respect to the sellers and attributes to this figure a bullish value.

descending triangle

The figure represents a symmetrical structure, which makes it difficult to interpret. In the third case, on the other hand, we speak of an ascending triangle, characterized by an upper line of flat demarcation and a line, the lower, ascending line. This pattern indicates a greater strength of the uptrend and is often found during an uptrend

Regardless of the configuration, whether symmetrical, ascending or descending, it is possible to calculate the target of the figure, i.e. the level that prices should reach in the phase following the breakout.

This is calculated by projecting, from the breaking point, the "base" of the triangle, i.e. the maximum width that the figure recorded during its formation.

The sixth figure in question concerns the formation of broadening.

Broadening

This represents a rather rare figure, classified as a variant of the triangle but which presents a contrary opening, with divergent trend lines. It is a figure that occurs at the end of a trend, usually bullish.

The dynamics of the volumes are different from that of the triangles, as the volume gradually expands together with the increase in price oscillation.

The seventh figure that we are going to examine concerns the diamond.

Diamond

Also, the diamond as an inversion figure is one of the rarest and one of the least simple to detect. Graphically the diamond is formed by a double-figure composed of a first half that recalls the shape of a broadening from a second half that resembles a symmetrical triangle.

A diamond can present itself in two circumstances:

- at the end of an uptrend;
- at the end of a bearish trend;

In the first case, it takes the name of "Diamond Top," vice versa we would be facing a "Diamond Bottom."

The figure does not always develop symmetrically. Often, the second half is prolonged in time more than the first one did.

By its nature, the diamond needs very dynamic market phases. The figure of the Diamond can also occur during simple breaks of the trend.

For this reason, it is easier to find the diamond at the peak of an upward trend before a bearish reversal rather than the other way around. diamond

The dynamics of volumes go hand in hand with that of prices. That is, if volumes increase, prices increase, in the second half. However, prices fall and consequently also volumes.

There are 4 basic elements to identify the training:

an initial phase of price expansion;

a maximum;

a minimum;

a phase of price contraction;

The pattern is only complete when the support or resistance line breaks and a pullback to the violated trend line does not always occur.

The minimum price target is equal to the maximum vertical distance between the two extreme parts of the figure projected at the bottom (or at the top) with respect to the breaking point of the support or resistance.

It is possible, even for the diamond, to calculate a target price.

It is sufficient to project the maximum width of the figure and project it starting from the point where the breakout occurred.

In the event that it is configured as a continuation figure, it is also possible to derive a second target, projecting the width of the movement that preceded the beginning of the diamond, from the point of the final breakout. diamond breaking points

The eighth figure we examine will be a figure difficult enough to examine and represents the rounding and spike.

Rounding and Spike

This represents one of the many figures of inversions, which presents itself as a slow and gradual movement on the lows that will first have a slight downward, then lateral and then shows a growing movement.

The pattern is one of the slowest of all the graphic analysis and is usually identifiable on longer-term charts.

It is really difficult to establish the precise moment in which the figure can be considered complete, if not after the first substantial rises. More difficult, it will be to identify upward targets.

Spike is also very special. The figures in question show, without any transition period, a sudden reversal of the quotations. An inversion accompanied by an explosion of volumes.

Due to its characteristics, the figure in question is difficult to identify in advance.

Double Top and Double Bottom

Also, this falls into the categories of the inversion figures, which we remember are particular graphic figures that announce an inversion of the current trend. The figure in question turns out to be a very common figure in graphic analysis and together with other figures, the double bottom and double top figures are among the most common and recognizable formations.

We explain briefly in two essential steps, its operation;

1. The double minimum is at the peak of a bearish trend and is configured as a minimum, a subsequent rebound and a subsequent fallback to the level of the previous minimum. The ascent that follows, if it breaks on the upside and with volumes, the previous maximum, leads to the completion of the figure. The pattern, due to its shape, is also called a formation in W. Volumes are growing during the formation of the first minimum, down in the following rebound, and then increase again during the upward movement that completes the figure.

Basically, therefore, the double minimum is realized, following a clear bearish trend, in which prices test twice a price threshold, but without being able to overcome it. This determines the realization of two minimums slightly spaced over time. Double minimum and double maximum.

1. Also, the characteristics of the double maximum are the same, but the pattern has a secularly opposite development. The double top is at the height of an uptrend and is configured as a maximum, a consequent fall and a subsequent rebound towards the previous maximum.

The double maximum is achieved when, following a sharp uptrend, prices test twice a price threshold, but without being able to overcome it, determining the formation of two maximums. Volumes are growing at the formation of the first rise, remaining lower in the formation of the second maximum and then increasing conspicuously at the time of the piercing of the traceable line starting from the previous minimum.

In both figures, it is possible to observe a return of prices to the level of completion of the pattern, in a pullback similar to that of the head and shoulders that we will see later, before the definitive start of the new trend, bullish in the double minimum and bearish in the double maximum. Small volumes accompany this pullback.

The measurement of the minimum upward (or downward) target is calculated by calculating the distance between the line joining the two minima (or the two maxima) and the first maximum (or minimum) relative and projecting this value from the upward drilling point or downward.

Having the Right Mindset for Trading

Before you proceed with learning the technical elements for how you can successfully swing trade with options, I want to pause for a moment to provide you with some crucial mindset tips for making your trades successful. When it comes to trading, your mindset can either be the weapon you use to win or the weapon you point against yourself in a battle of self-sabotage.

People who are not in the right frame of mind when trading has a tendency to let fear and frustration rule their judgment, which can lead to them making poor trade moves that ultimately result in losses. If you want to hedge yourself against risk, you need to hedge yourself against your emotions too and learn how to trade logically, rationally, and objectively.

Although there are many different mindset strategies you can use to help you improve your trade skills and make better quality trades, the following five are the most important for beginners. Please take these tips seriously, as they can make or break you in the stock market and you always want everything working in favor of your success.

Beginners are especially at risk of making emotional trades based on the fact that there is a large amount of excitement and uncertainty swirling around when you are new to trading. If you get caught in this emotional state, however, your earliest experiences making trades may not be positive and could even put you off of the idea of trading altogether, solely because your mind was not in the right place.

Stay Committed, Be Persistent

You must be committed to your trades and stay persistent in your desire to win if you are going to be successful with trading any form of stocks.

Without commitment and persistence, you are going to find yourself struggling, as you will be unwilling to stay focused on what it takes to succeed.

Those who are not committed and persistent fall behind on their research and conduct low-quality tech analysis readings which can result in low-quality trades that lead to excessive losses. In the options market specifically, you might also find profitable options expiring before you act on them because you have not remained consistent in your approach to your trades.

A great way for you to stay committed and persistent in your trades is through setting a goal for yourself which will clearly outline the reason for why you have begun trading in the first place.

When you have a goal, you know what you are set to achieve and you have a strong reason for why you need to stay committed and persistent so that you can reach that goal.

I strongly encourage you to outline a goal for yourself before you get started so that you can leverage your goal to help you stay committed and focused throughout your trades.

Some great examples of goals include:

- Pay off debt and accumulate a nest egg for yourself/your family
- Set aside funds for your children to go to college
- Afford to travel and enjoy the world
- Replace your salary with profits from trades so you can quit your day job

- Buy a house or investment property with your profits

Pick a goal that is relevant to what you want for yourself and your life so that you are motivated by it, as this is an important step in making your goal worth going for.

Be Aware of Your Emotions

Self-awareness, particularly around your emotions, is a strong asset for you to have when it comes to trading. When you are trading, you need to be aware of your emotions surrounding your trades so that you can avoid letting fear, frustration, anger, or uncertainty rule your trades. People who trade fearfully or with frustration tend to make decisions that are not founded in logic, which can result in massive and unnecessary losses incurred. As a result, they may grow even more fearful or frustrated with trading because they are not seeing the results they desire, which makes it even more challenging for them to make successful trades going forward.

Rather than starting that cycle, it is better to become aware of your emotions and practice staying aware of them during every trade you make.

The way that I manage my emotions and stress during trades comes in the form of a quick and simple self-check which I make periodically throughout the trading process. Generally, whenever I conduct tech analysis, choose my position, execute a trade, and complete a trade, I engage in an emotional check to see how I am doing. If I discover that I am feeling fearful or uncertain, or even frustrated, I manage my emotions first. Then, once I am feeling more balanced, I make my trade decision. This way, I can guarantee that every decision I make is founded in logic and reasoning, not fear and frustration.

Always Make Decisions Founded in Logic

Elaborating on my previous point, it is crucial that every decision you make is always founded in logic and reasoning. It can be surprisingly easy to engage in trades based off of how your emotions are feeling, or even based off of what you are hearing out in the world around the topic of trades. You might find yourself noticing that whenever you hear about the market in the news or in trade circles that you spend time in that you feel persuaded to change your mind based off of what you are hearing from other people.

While it is important to take their information into consideration and use it to help you educate yourself, it is important that you never make a decision based off of what someone else has told you, or based off of your emotions. Instead, always conduct *your own* research to validate this information to ensure that you are making your decisions based off on logic and reasoning.

In today's society, it can be easy to get swept away by what other people are telling you. When I was brand new to trading, I tended to doubt myself and trust others' judgment anytime I was engaged in groups where people who had more experience than me were trading. I assumed that because they had been trading longer, they had greater experience, and therefore, what they said must ultimately be true, which lead to me making some trade moves that I did not validate with my own research.

Most of those fell through with losses, which made me realize the importance of this. Make sure that you hedge yourself against this risk by always validating everything with thorough research and tech analysis to ensure that you are always making the best decisions possible.

Stay Humble

Regardless of how and where you trade, the stock market is a place where you need to stay humble. Just like fear and uncertainty can push you to make poor trade deals, being overconfident can also lead to you making poor trade deals. People who are overconfident in the market tend to lose respect for how volatile the market can be and forget that just like you can profit plenty, you can also lose plenty. This can lead to terrible decisions and cocky trading, which may ultimately lead to potentially devastating losses in your trade deals.

Staying humble is not just to protect your pride, it is also to protect your trade deals to ensure that you are always hedging yourself against possible risks and losses.

You must always thoroughly conduct every step of tech analysis and trade research before getting involved, even if you have been on a winning streak. Do not roll the dice or gamble with your trades or assume that you know exactly how to win every single time just because you have won a few trades in a row or earned yourself massive profits. Stay humble, or the market will humble you.

Be Open to Learning

The final mindset note I will leave you with is that you need to be open to learning. As you get involved with trading, you will find a strategy that works for you and that you will want to stick with that strategy because it is familiar and comfortable. That is great, and everyone should be on the lookout for finding a way that works for them. After all, this is a strong way to ensure that you feel confident in the decisions that you are making so that you can make strong deals.

With that being said, you should always be open to learning and evolving your strategy so that you can do even better over time.

Continually learning is not just about improving your strategy either, but it is also about staying up with general trader trends. Trader trends are different from market trends in that we are not discussing what direction the market is moving in, but rather the strategies that traders are using to trade on the market itself.

Keeping up with these trends ensures that you are always trading similarly to how other successful traders are trading, which improves your chances at generating success with your trades.

The Secret of Profitable Trading

The most important thing in trading, what professionals traders call the "secret" is not having the ability to recognize when a trade is going bad , most if not all traders know when they should exit the trade, the getting out part is what is hard for the 90% of traders who fail. The key here is having the discipline to cut a trade off when it is not working. It is that simple. Developing the habit (which can be found here on how to develop successful habits: click the link *HABITS: How to Build any Habit and Make it Stick*)of getting out of trades when you are told to by the stock is easy, listening to that advice is the key. If the trade is not doing what you expect, get out immediately. Trying to make the trade work is not going to help you and only reinforces horrible trading habits. This is what separates successful traders from traders that never make it. This goes back to anticipating what you think the trade is going to do and reacting (putting the trade on) once it starts doing what you anticipated.

This type of trading will save you from being in trades and not knowing what to do. We are all about preserving capital to take advantage of the large moves in the market. We want to be a part of the moves not trying to anticipate the moves and making sure we are trading when everything is in our favor.

Trading is not a race, it is not a marathon either. I would consider it more of high intensity interval training (HIIT), there will be times when you lay at rest waiting for the opportune time to take advantage of a situation and then there will be times why you will need laser focus on a specific trade and you will have to give it everything you have to extract the most profit from that trade. This focus is necessary for it to work.

Smaller Account Trading vs. Large Account Trading

Small Account Trading

Working with a smaller account, there is extreme risk. You cannot afford to take multiple large losses in a row. Your main objective is to take the losses when they come, small losses do not hurt your account here. They will actually start to give you a sort of discipline and allow you to stay in the market longer when a trade will come your way that will make up for the losses you sustained. When taking a trade with a smaller account you are looking for a trade that will give you more than you are risking. Risk: Reward, so for a trade that is 1:3 this would be a great trade, you can make the money you loss on three trades back with one trade. *Working with a smaller account doesn't provide you with a lot of flexibility but it teaches you more about the discipline of trading than anything else.* This is why I recommend day trading with the minimum $500 that SureTrader allows. You will definitely learn discipline this way. When you are disciplined as a trader making profits with a smaller account or larger account is the same, the difference is the size of the position. Small account trading doesn't necessarily mean you have to trade a small position. With certain brokers, the leverage sometimes goes up to 1:6 which means, depending on the size of your account you can get into some pretty large trades relative to the equity in your account. When trading a smaller account the issue you run into is being able to take enough size on the ticker you are trading to make a decent profit to cover commissions. This typically means that you need to take all of your size on the first entry, which means that you need to be right more often that you are wrong. With this type of trading, discipline is the main factor to success and being able to identify the proper setups. Trading with smaller accounts vs. larger accounts means you need to be reactive instead of anticipating. We will go over reactive trading vs anticipatory trading later. For example, let's say you are starting with a trading account of approximately $3,000 and with the broker that I am trading with, that will give you approximately $18,000 in trading capital. Below are the break downs on the levels of stocks that I typically trade and the money that can be made on the 1st base through home run scenarios:

Large Account Trading

The strategies remain the same, the major difference is the larger account trading and the smaller account trading is the size of positions you can trade and the amount of trades you can put on at once and the size of position you can put on at once. Trading a larger account gives you the flexibility to make more money faster and also allows you to make more mistakes along the way. When trading with a larger account, you can make larger mistakes but I strongly advise against trading with the total size of an account. I would trade or restrict your trading to a smaller portion of your account until you learn how to trade with the discipline you need to make the money you want. As an example let's say you have $10,000 in your account and you are using the same broker as before, let's look at the chart to see what the profit potential can be:

As you can see the profits are multiplied 6 fold as well as the amount of money you can lose. We all know that trading goes both ways here. The money you stand to make is also the money you can lose depending on what your risk level is and where you place your stops when reviewing the charts. This is why stops are so important. With large account trading there is also an added benefit, you can size into a position as it gyrates in the direction you expect it to go. There is obviously more flexibility when trading a larger account, the ability to absorb losses is huge here. Still the discipline remains the same, or you will be back to trading a smaller account very soon.

Mental Stops vs. System Order Stops

I have tried both approaches and there are drawbacks to both. Mental stops are at your mercy and you need extreme discipline to make these work. I have used mental stops before and have had great success and failure with them. One of the biggest failures I have had with mental stops is not getting out when I was supposed to and letting the stock run more than it should. The success that I have had with them is being able to put on a trade and knowing exactly how much I am risking on a trade and letting the trade work. This approach has given me the greatest amount of profit. Actually placing stops in the system is a great thing, if the stop actually triggered when it was supposed to. The issue I have had in the past is the stop didn't trigger and the stock ran right through the stop, which the purpose of the stop was to stop this from happening. There are all sorts of reasons, if you are going to use a mental stop, I warn against it if you are just starting out. I would suggest using a system stop (Stop Limit) to make sure you get out close to the price that you want and nothing else. This will give you more comfort in knowing that you have predetermined your risk tolerance for that specific trade and in doing so, you know how much money you are risking. Once the trade starts working in your favor you should start moving your stop down according to how the stock is acting. Depending on the activity of the stock, I would move it down it 10 to 12 cent increments to lock in some profit on the trade. This will help you build your account and also help you take profit once the stock has a bounce which they will inevitably do. This will also get you out of stocks that have more downside, so use this method with caution. For example if you have not locked in any profit at the 1st base level, consider selling some and allowing the stock to bounce before moving your stop down to that level, once it moves to that level and beyond, place your stop at the 1st base mark and allow the trade to work in your favor for the rest of your position.

Commandments of Swing Trading

Some of the most experienced swing traders of 2019 like to focus on what has become known as the 11 commandments of swing trading. Popular trader, Melvin Pasternak, developed this list and discusses it after his trading classes.

1. Make Sure to Have Long Strengths and Short Weaknesses

There are two periods that you should be looking for when you are taking on a trade. The first period is known as bull and the second period is known as bear. You need to be able to identify these periods when you get into the market because this will let you know what the market conditions are like for that time.

When you look at the bull market condition, you are looking at an increasing market. The stock trends are on an upward trend, which they have been on for a good period of time. This proves that the levels of the economy are high and you should spend your time looking for longer trades.

When the market's condition is focused on bearishness, this means that the stocks are on a downward trend. The prices of stocks are dropping and many traders believe that this is the spiral that they will see in some stocks for a period of time. Bear conditions happen when the economy isn't doing very well. This is normally during points of economic recession and when unemployment is high. When you notice the bear conditions, you will want to focus on short trades as this will limit your risk of loss, especially if the downward trend continues.

2. The Overall Direction of the Market and Your Trade Should be Aligned

This is one reason research is important. You not only want to research when you are starting your swing trade profession, but you also want to continue your research. In fact, every day that you sit down in front of your desk, is a day that you will be doing research. One of these reasons is because you have to make sure to research and analyze every stock. This will help you determine whether you should purchase the stock or not.

When you are focusing on your research for a particular stock, one of the main focuses should be does the stock match the overall direction of the market? When it comes to the stock market, you will find that it's either on an upward or downward spiral. You will want to match your trade with this direction.

3. Always Look at the Long-Term Charts

One of the biggest mistakes that beginner traders often make is that they will only focus on the short-term charts when they are looking into a stock. Many experienced traders feel that this is the wrong course of action as you should have a better idea of what the trend of the stock has done over at least a six-month period. Of course, you can always go longer than six months.

You should start with the chart that will give you a couple of weeks. From there, you will want to make sure you go over the chart and notice every single detail. There is nothing that you should miss during the analysis of your chart. After you have looked at the first couple of weeks, then you can dive more into a long-term chart, such as the six-month chart. Again, follow the same microscopic process you did with the previous chart. Do your best not to miss anything. In fact, some traders will often create an excel spreadsheet where they can list everything they have to view in the chart and even write down information. This is a great piece of advice for any beginner.

4. Do Your Best Not to Enter Near the End of the Trade

Once you start to get into the stock market, you will notice a trend when it comes to traders. You will find that the stock market is busy within the first hour because there are so many traders who are buying new stocks for the day. You will then notice that the stock market begins to get quiet around the 11:00 hour because people are either holding on to their stocks or closed out for the day. However, about the last hour, which starts around 3:00 pm, you will notice the stock market picks up again as people, especially day traders, sell all their stocks and close out.

As a swing trader, you might not buy and sell stocks every day. Unlike day traders, you can hold your stocks for a few days to about a week or two. However, there are a few traders that are not allowed to do this as it would cause them too much loss.

Another reason people enter into trades earlier rather than later is because this can give you the most profit, especially if you find a stock that is hitting an upward trend. On top of this, you will have less risk to worry about if you enter a trade early. Doing your best to cut down on risk is always something traders focus on, even if they don't mind taking risks.

5. Track a Consistent Group of Stocks

Just like every trader is different, every stock is different. This is why it is important to not focus on jumping from one stock to the next. Instead, as you are learning the tricks and strategies of swing trading, you will want to start getting an idea of what kind of stocks you like. Every stock has its own personality and once you catch on to that specific personality, trading will become easier if you stick to groups of stocks that are similar.

One reason for this is because you will most likely be able to use the same strategy for all of your stocks. This can help you when it comes to learning techniques and strategies. It is easier to stick to one strategy because there are so many tiny details about swing trading you need to remember, the human brain can only hold so much information.

Another reason for this is because this allows you to be able to manage a certain amount of stocks consistently. If you are a full-time swing trader, you will find this system will give you less stress, keep your focus, and increase confidence in your abilities. Of course, all this will help you keep your right state of mind as a trader.

6. Always Have a Clear Plan

Whenever you enter a trade, you will want to make sure that you have a clear plan of action. This plan will most likely be your trading plan; however, this is known to change from time to time as traders start to learn and grow with their profession. While this is great as it means you are becoming a more successful trader, you will also want to make sure that you continue to update and adjust your plan as you need to.

Before you enter any trade, it is best to go through your plan and make sure that it will work with that stock. If you find it won't, then you will need to either adjust your trading plan or choose a stock that will fit your trading plan better.

You will want to make sure that everything is including in this plan from your entry to your exit. You will want to make sure that you have all the key points and details down. On top of this, you will also want to make sure that you have a stop-loss strategy in place so you can quickly let go of that stock through a trade and walk away from losing a large amount of money. Remember, when you decide the stop-loss strategy is the best course of action, it will happen quickly. In fact, trading is a very faced-paced business, which is another reason making sure you always have a clear plan of action is a commandment.

7. Always Integrate Fundamentals into Your Technical Analysis

While I will discuss technical analysis later in this book, one of the 11 commandments of swing trading is to make sure that you integrate fundamentals into your analysis. If you have looked into day trading, you will know a bit about fundamentals and more about technical analysis. However, when it comes to swing trading, fundamentals becomes just as important as technical analysis. The main reason for this is because you hold your stocks longer than a few minutes to a few hours.

8. Make Sure to Master the Psychological side of Swing Trading

As you will see later in this book, there is a lot of psychology that goes into swing trading. In fact, psychology goes into any type of trading, but it is more crucial when it comes to swing traders. While part of this is about keeping the right mindset, the other part comes from the overall experience of swing trading. There are a lot of factors, such as making mistakes, learning, and losing that can affect your psyche throughout your day. For example, if you take a loss you might find that you feel like a failure after you have closed out your day. This can affect your personal life as well as your working life. It is extremely important to make sure that you have a healthy frame of mind and not just the right mindset when you are a trader.

9. Try Putting the Odds in Your Favor

Sometimes you will look at a trade and wonder if you will be able to make a profit on it. This is why it is important to use technical analysis with every trade. However, even if you feel that you might not be able to make a profit, this doesn't mean that you walk away from the trade. In fact, you can take this time to work on putting the odds in your favor. While this means you might end up risking a profit, trading is always full of risks. In fact, you will never be able to fully eliminate risks. Therefore, there are times where you have to take the leap and use certain techniques in order to try to work the trade into your favor.

One way to do this is by having a target price, which should always be a part of your target plan. This price will tell you when you should quickly turn to sell or trade the stock and when you should hold on to it for a bit longer. No matter what the market conditions are, you always want to stick to your target price. Therefore, you want to make sure that you complete your technical analysis to the best of your abilities before you go forward with your trading plan.

Furthermore, it is important to not only assess the chart once but also to reassess the chart. This means that you don't just analyze the chart before you take on the trade as you will continue to look at the chart and see what the stock's trend is doing in real-time. This means that you will notice the stock price increase and decreasing throughout the time you are analyzing.

10. Trade in Harmony with the Trend Time Frames

When it comes to the stock market, there are three types of trend time frames. The longest time frame is a year. The intermediate time frame is about three months. The shortest time frame is less than a month. When you are a swing trader, you will typically focus on the intermediate and short-term time frames. However, there are traders who have stated that they have looked at trends as far back as six months. Typically, swing traders don't have to focus on the longer time frame because they are considered to be short-term traders. At the same time, swing traders need to do more than just look at the short-term trend lines.

In fact, many expert swing traders will tell beginners that if they only focus on the short-term time frame, they are more likely to make mistakes. While you can always get a good sense of what the stock is doing with the short-term time frame, this can also limit you. The stock market is a very unpredictable place. This means that the further you look back, the better your idea will be about the type of trend that goes with the stock. The key is to heavily focus on the short-term trends and then do an analysis of the intermediate trends.

11. Make Sure to Use Multiple Indicators and Not Create Isolation

Sometimes traders will often feel that they only need to use one tool to give them an idea of what stock will give them a profitable trade and what stock won't. You should never do this. You always want to make sure that you use multiple tools and that these tools give you consistent results. For example, you might use a strategy, candlestick chart, volume, and other tools in order to find out that your trade will be profitable.

One of the reasons this is important is because it helps you limit your risks. The more tools you have that give you consistent results, the more likely you are to be able to make a profit.

The Top Mistakes That Beginners Make

As a beginner, there are a lot of things that you need to learn to do well with swing trading. Learning all the strategies, learning how to read the charts and making smart decisions when it comes to picking out stocks to work with can be a challenge. As you are getting used to the whole process, it can take some time and effort, and you are likely to make some mistakes along the way.

These mistakes are pretty normal when you are a beginner, but no beginner wants to deal with them. They want to be able to make as much money as possible, without losing a lot of money as they start to learn how things work. This chapter focuses on some of the top mistakes that a lot of beginners make and some of the things that you can do to avoid these common mistakes.

Let the emotions get in the way

One mistake that almost all beginners will make is that they let their emotions get in the way of their decision making. They see that they are about to lose out on a trade or they see that the profits will keep reaching a higher value, and they want to stay in the market longer, despite what all their research and their strategy told them before. This will end up disastrous and is one of the leading reasons that beginners lose so much money and end up having to stop at day trading.

You need to learn how to keep the emotions out of the game. If you are a highly emotional person, swing trading is not going to be the best option for you to try out because things can change in an instant. The good news is that there are a few techniques that you can use to help keep the emotions out of the game so you can reduce your risk and increase your chances of profit.

First, make sure that you use stop points and that you stick with them. These stop points will ensure that you enter and exit the trade at the right times to either limit your losses or to help limit the risk that you have while gaining a profit. They aren't always full proof, but if you stick with them, you are less likely to have issues later on. Picking a good strategy, asking for advice, and really doing your research before you begin are all good ways to ensure you can keep the emotions out of your trading.

Forget to use stop points

The stop points will be so important when you start out as a swing trader. These points will tell you when to get out of the market, whether the market is going up or down and can reduce your risk. You need to have a stop loss point, which is the point you will get out of the market if you lose so much money, and you need a stop profit point, which is where you will get out of the market once you earn a certain profit.

Both of these are important to ensure you cut down on your risk and that you make as much money as possible in the process. For the stop loss point, you are figuring out how much money you are comfortable with losing in the market. Once the market goes down to this point, you need to get out. It is highly likely that the market will keep going down and if you don't get out at your stop loss point, you will potentially lose a lot of money in the process. This takes the emotions out of the game. You simply see that the stop point was reached and cut your losses until the next trade.

You also need to have a stop point for the profits that you want to earn. This may seem silly because you want to earn as much profit as you possibly can with each trade. But emotions can come into play here again too. Without the stop point, you may end up staying in the market too long, and make some costly mistakes. The market can turn around just as quickly as it went up, and if you are still in the market, you may lose all your earnings instead of gaining anything.

For this stop point, figure out what you can realistically make on the trade. Where do you think the market for your stock will go over the next few days based on the trend that you are setting? Put the stop point there and then as soon as the market reaches that point, you will take your earnings and withdraw from the market.

Putting in more money than you can afford to lose

With any investment that you work with, you need to be careful about the losses that you are dealing with. If you take on too much risk, you will end up losing all your money and never getting a chance to give it another try. Coming up with a good risk to reward ratio will help to limit your losses, but you also must make sure that you never put in more than you are willing to lose.

A good place to start is to put some savings behind for your swing trades. Never use money that you would need for rent, food, and other necessities. The second you do this, you bring the emotions into the game, and you are more likely to lose it all. Starting a savings account right now with the money you can use for swing trading allows you to have a little cushion without having to eat up all the money you need for other things.

When you are using the extra money, rather than money that you really need elsewhere, you are ensuring that you will spend it wisely. You won't stay in a trade too long in the hopes of recovering that money. No one wants to lose money along the way when they are trading, but it is much easier to cut your losses when it was just a little savings rather than if that money was your rent payment for the month.

Not understanding your strategy

If you do not understand the strategy that you are using, it can be impossible for you to get results when you get started with swing trading. Your strategy will outline exactly how you will behave in each trade situation. It will tell you how to look at the charts, how to pick out the stocks, when to enter the market, and when to exit the market. Each strategy has the potential to be successful, but you need to understand the strategy and use it properly.

When you get started in swing trading, it is always best to start with a simple strategy. Yes, there are some more complex ones that may sound fun, but since you are already learning about the market and how it works, why add in more complications with a hard strategy. There are a lot of great strategies that are simple, and some even designed for the beginner, that will make you just as much money as the more complex strategies, without all the work.

Picking a strategy is really important when it comes to doing well in swing trading. Before you pick out one, make sure to read through them all and fully understand what you will need to do to make it successful. You want one that is effective and easy to follow, as well as one that you will not want to switch out of in the middle of the trade. There is nothing wrong with trying out different strategies to see which one you like the best in between your trades, but if you switch strategies while in the same trade, you are setting yourself up for failure.

Not having the right tools

As a trader, you need to have some of your own tools in place if you would like to get started with swing trading. This can be a very difficult method when it comes to investing, and without the right tools, you will miss out on some important information that can help you see trends and make smart decisions along the way.

The first place to go for some tools is to talk to your broker. Often the broker will have a variety of unique tools that they can give to you as part of their fees. If you don't know how to use some of these tools, make sure to ask questions and learn how to make it all work or you will miss out.

You can also bring in some of your own tools to the game as well. Find charts about the market, look online, and ask questions. Remember, the best way to notice a trend is when the same information starts to show up on more than one chart or tool so always strive to have as many of these tools available as possible.

Following others rather than learning your own way

When you first get started, it can be tempting to find a mentor or a group and then just follow along exactly with what they do each time. This is really tempting if you see that they are making a lot of money and you want to join and make that money as well. But in the long run, no one knows the trading style that you like, and there are times when even an advanced mentor will get things wrong.

Instead of following along blindly with what someone else tell you, it is better to learn your own way. There is nothing wrong with talking to a mentor and others who have been in the market for some time, but you need to learn your own methods, your own strategies, and how you want to behave in the market. This will help you to stay on track with your trades and will ensure that you don't get misled by others who may not have your best interests at heart.

Not cutting your losses

Even the best swing traders will make mistakes at times. They will misread the market, they will try out a new strategy that doesn't work for them, or the market just doesn't behave in the manner that they had hoped. And when this happens, the trader will lose out on their money. As a beginner, it is more likely that you will earn a loss at some point. The important thing is to learn how to cut your losses, rather than staying too long in the market.

Some beginners will see that they are losing money on one of their trades and so they will try to regain that money. Even with the market going down, and no signs of reversal, they will stay in the market and hope that things will reverse. This is dangerous because it results in you staying in the market way too long and you will lose out on way too much money in the process.

Instead of sticking with a market that is not working in your favor, it is much better to learn how to cut your losses. Pick out an amount that you are comfortable with losing if the market does not go the way that you would like, put a stop point there, and then withdraw from the market as soon as you reach that point. This will help you to limit your losses and can give you more opportunities to try another trade in the future.

Conclusion

Congratulations for making it to the end of this book! I know it was a lot of information for you to take in, so this is really an accomplishment in your swing trading career!

One of the goals of this book was to give you a start on your swing trading career. Not only did I want to explain the key concepts of financial trading. Because this is considered to be a foundation when it comes to trading, I didn't want to leave this information out of the book. On top of this, it was important to explain to you the difference between trading and investing. There are a lot of people who get into trading when they believed they were going to be investing money instead of trading stocks in order to gain a profit. Because these two topics are different, it is important to make sure you want to be a trader and not an investor before you go too far into your research for swing trading.

Another major point of this book was to give you a concise beginner's guide about swing trading which touched on a variety of topics. Instead of you having to read dozens more articles and a few books about swing trading, I wanted to give you a way that you can place one book in your device to turn to when you need a refresher about swing trading. On top of this, I wanted you to be able to bring this book to your friends who are interested in swing trading and show them this beginner's guide, so they can get all the information required before opening their account with a broker.

As you have realized by this point, swing trading is not the easiest career; however, when it comes to the stock market, there is no easy career. It doesn't matter if you decide on swing trading, become a buy and hold investor, or get into day trading you will find that each one of these areas have their own challenges. However, you will soon come to find that they each have their own advantages as well. You should already to be able to pick out a few advantages to becoming a swing trader. For example, you could one day be able to trade without the assistance of a broker. On top of this, you have been able to get a sneak peak of the many online communities for swing traders. Once you decide to join an online community or two, you will realize how enjoyable swing trading is.

You should also understand what simulation trading is and how important it is to make sure you complete this type of trading before you start trading for money. You should also not only understand risks which are associated in swing trading but also have an idea on how to decrease these risks once you start swing trading. Of course, this is one reason you want to make sure to practice simulation trading at first. As stated before, simulation trading will help you make sure that you understand the risks and the strategies which are associated with swing trading.

By now you should not only clearly understand what swing trading is, but also what the average time fame is for a swing trader. You should be able to remember the 11 commandments of swing trading, techniques, what the right mindset is when you are trading, know a variety of tips to help you get on your way, and also understand the many mistakes that other swing traders have made.

Furthermore, you should be able to explain how a day will go for a full-time swing trader, be able to explain the two different types of stock market conditions, and the art of short selling.

On top of all the information you need to know about being a swing trader, you also know how to get started with researching as much information as possible. On top of this, you have learned tips to help you become a better researcher, so you can gain the most out of your research time. It is important to keep these tips in mind as you will need to used them throughout your career. On top of this, you can also add your own tips, which will become useful when you begin to help other beginner swing traders in the next few years.

Thank you for not only purchasing this book but also reading it. I hope that you found it helpful in your swing trading journey. I wish you the best of luck! If you would be so kind, please take a minute to leave a review about my book. Thank you!

www.ingramcontent.com/pod-product-compliance
Lightning Source LLC
Chambersburg PA
CBHW070644220526
45466CB00001B/288